Ellis Island and Immigration for Kids

A HISTORY WITH 21 ACTIVITIES

JEAN DAIGNEAU

CHICAGO REVIEW PRESS

Copyright © 2022 by Jean Daigneau
All rights reserved
First edition
Published by Chicago Review Press, Incorporated
814 North Franklin Street
Chicago, Illinois 60610
ISBN 978-1-64160-468-0

Library of Congress Control Number: 2021946179

Cover and interior design: Sarah Olson
Cover images: *(front cover)* Annie Moore statue,
DeFacto/Wikimedia Commons; Main building at
Ellis Island, USA-Reiseblogger/Pixabay; White Star
Line postcard, courtesy of the Library of Congress;
Immigrants on the steerage deck of the *Germanic*,
courtesy of the Library of Congress; Sinaida Gruss-
man, courtesy of the US Holocaust Memorial
Museum; Mexican migrant workers, courtesy of the
Farm Security Administration, Library of Congress;
DACA supporteres at Washington, DC, Rena Schild/
Shutterstock; Notebook showing Dan Hi Loy, Chin
Hung, Noy Hen, and Lock Yan, California Histori-
cal Society; *(back cover)* Slovak woman and children,
Manuscripts and Archives Division, The New York
Public Library. (1906–1914); Handwritten poster from
the Women's March on Washington, 2017, courtesy of
the Collection of the Smithsonian National Museum
of African American History and Culture
Interior illustrations: Jim Spence

Printed in the United States of America
5 4 3 2 1

This book is dedicated to my dear, departed friend Jean Kreyche, who opened my eyes to the issues of the undocumented and who lived the Gospels every day of her life in service to others. Rest in peace, dear friend.

And to my grandparents—Dominic and Theresa Colpo and Federico and Carmela Pozzini—for taking a chance on a better life and making the journey to the US.

CONTENTS

Acknowledgments * vii

Time Line * viii

Introduction * xi

1 Castle Island: The Foundation for Ellis Island * 1
Pack for an Immigrant Journey * 3
Write a Letter Home * 6
Could You Survive? * 8

2 Ellis Island: A New Gateway to America * 11
Write a Poem to Welcome Immigrants * 14
Bake Italian *Mustasoles* * 19

3 Ellis Island: Island of Tears, Island of Joy * 23
Matching and Creating Medical Letters * 27
Make Your Money Count * 32

4 When It All Began * 35
How Beringia Disappeared * 38
Make a Whirligig * 43

5 A Great Migration Begins * 47
Photographing and Videotaping Family History * 51
Panning for Gold * 55

6 A New Country Confronts New Changes * 59
Create a Topographical Map * 64
Stow Away a Time Capsule * 68

7 Immigration Changes the United States Forever * 71
Branch Out and Create a Family Tree * 73
How Do Your Family Members Match Up? * 77

8 World Crises and the US Response ✳ 81

How Did Ethnicity Change? ✳ 86

Create an Immigration Poster ✳ 91

9 The United States Confronts Global Issues Again ✳ 93

Kids Count Too! ✳ 98

Let Your Voice Be Heard ✳ 102

10 Immigration in an Ever-Changing World ✳ 105

Sponsor an International Picnic ✳ 116

Make an Immigration Time Line ✳ 119

Glossary ✳ 120

Answers Revealed ✳ 122

Websites and Places to Visit ✳ 124

Notes ✳ 126

Selected Bibliography ✳ 128

Index ✳ 129

ACKNOWLEDGMENTS

MY SINCERE THANKS to my editor, Jerry Pohlen, for taking on this project and for his guidance getting this book from beginning to end. And special thanks to Assistant Project Editor Ben Krapohl and copyeditor Sharon Sofinski for all their suggested additions and deletions as well as catching things that I missed (read: mistakes) and making me look so darn good! My appreciation also to everyone at Chicago Review Press for their work. What an amazing team!

I can't find words enough to thank Dr. Alan Kraut, Distinguished Professor of History at American University in Washington, DC. His knowledge of immigration and his willingness to read my manuscript, make suggestions, and answer questions and e-mails made me look way more knowledgeable about the subject than I am.

So much love and appreciation goes out to my agent extraordinaire, Vicki Selvaggio. Without your support and encouragement, this journey would be infinitely harder, if not impossible, and a heck of a lot less fun!

Special thanks to the Jambies—Gloria Adams, Joan Arbogast, and LeeAnn Blankenship—along with Charlie Colman, editors extraordinaire, for their love and support and for catching mistakes, suggesting changes, and helping condense all my wordy thoughts. Thanks to the Jemelies—Emily Levin, Judith Leisenring, and Janice Stefko—the best cheerleading squad around. Love you, all!

Kudos to the librarians, curators, digital collections coordinators, government employees, sculptors, photographers, and others who made my work finding photos much easier.

To my activity betas, Ryan Walter-Daigneau and Tessa and June Daigneau, I appreciate your coming to Noni's aid and letting me know what worked and what didn't. And that includes Pat and Fred Wygant, Ben Daigneau, Nick Daigneau, Simon Walter-Daigneau, and Izzy Abner for guiding them along. To my neighborhood betas, I send my deepest appreciation as well: Zoe Mistur and her parents Mike Mistur and Frances Penney, and Asa and Quinn Turnidge, and their parents Katie Strand and Jason Turnidge. Your enthusiasm and help with activities was much appreciated.

Adolfo Duarte and Noman Biswas, thanks for sharing your stories. And special thanks to Jean and Mike Kreyche for their support and connections to the immigrant community. Jean, I wish I would have told you this before your unexpected and untimely passing. Thank you both for opening my eyes so many years ago to issues that I knew nothing about.

And, as always, to my kids and grands for their love and support, especially during this last challenging year.

TIME LINE

1585 Roanoke colony established

1607 Jamestown established in the colony of Virginia

1609-1610 Winter called the "starving time" at Jamestown

1609-1775 First immigration wave

1798 Alien Enemies Act passed

1819 Steerage Act passed

1830-1860 Second immigration wave

January 24, 1848 Gold discovered at Sutter's Creek, California

1855 Carriage of Passengers Act passed

August 1, 1855 Castle Garden immigration station opened at Battery Park in Manhattan

1862 Homestead Act signed

April 1862 Confederate Draft Act signed

March 3, 1863 Civil War Military Draft Act signed

July 13, 1863 Draft Riots

1864 Act to Encourage Immigration signed

1875 Page Act enacted

1880-1920 Third immigration wave

1882 Chinese Exclusion Act enacted

May 4, 1886 Haymarket Riot

1890 Federal Bureau of Immigration established

Castle Garden closed

April 11, 1890 Ellis Island, in New York Bay, designated immigration station location

January 1, 1892 Ellis Island opened

June 15, 1897 Fire at Ellis Island

1907 Immigration Act of 1907 passed

April 17, 1907 Ellis Island experienced record arrivals

January 21, 1910 Angel Island opened in San Francisco Bay

1917 Immigration Act of 1917 enacted

June 3, 1921 Immigration Act of 1921 enacted

1924 Border Patrol established

Immigration Act of 1924 enacted

1929-1939 Repatriation drives occurred

1933 Immigration and Naturalization Service established

August 12, 1940 Fire at Angel Island

February 19, 1942 Japanese internment begun

1942 Bracero Program enacted

1943 Chinese Exclusion Act repealed

June 25, 1948 Displaced Persons Act signed

1952 Immigration and Naturalization Act of 1952 enacted

1953 Refugee Relief Act enacted

Summer 1954 Operation Wetback begun

November 12, 1954 Ellis Island closed

1962 Migration and Refugee Assistance Act passed

May 11, 1965 Ellis Island designated part of the Statue of Liberty National Monument

October 3, 1965 Immigration and Naturalization Act of 1965 signed

1965 and later Fourth immigration wave

1980 Refugee Act signed

1982 Statue of Liberty–Ellis Island Centennial Commission established

November 6, 1986 Immigration Reform and Control Act signed

September 9, 1990 Ellis Island reopened

1990 Immigration Act passed

September 30, 1996 Illegal Immigrant Reform and Immigrant Responsibility Act signed

2002 Department of Homeland Security created

2003 Immigration under the control of the US Citizenship and Immigration Services

2012 Consideration of Deferred Action for Childhood Arrivals (DACA) program established

2017 DACA program ended

January 2020 Coronavirus pandemic outbreak reported

INTRODUCTION

———

ROSY-CHEEKED 17-YEAR-OLD Annie Moore's 12-day trip from County Cork in Ireland was ending. For Annie and her brothers, long days in hot, crowded, and stuffy accommodations below deck—called **steerage**—along with 145 other passengers would be a thing of the past. As she felt the SS *Nevada* ply through the waters toward New York Harbor, she couldn't help but notice the Statue of Liberty. Lady Liberty was a welcoming sight.

The next day, January 1, 1892, was a day to remember. Annie and her brothers, Anthony and Phillip, would finally be reunited with their parents who had sailed to the United States the year before to establish a home and find work. When the gangplank lowered, Annie tripped her way across it and into the **immigration** station. As the first **immigrant** to set foot on Ellis Island, she had no idea she had just stepped into history.

Immigrants waiting to be transferred, October 30, 1912. *Courtesy of the Library of Congress*

Castle Island:
The Foundation for Ellis Island

—

"Dear Sister, do be careful on the streets [on the way]. When you arrive at Castle Garden telegraph me. Stay in Castle Garden until I come and fetch you. When you get here, you will not be digging for potatoes or pitching hay."

—Johann Bonkowski, Polish immigrant, April 26, 1891

[Note: This letter was dated one year after the Castle Garden immigration center closed.]

When people think of immigration and the United States, New York's Ellis Island often comes to mind. Opened in 1892, the Ellis Island immigration station welcomed as many as 12 million people until it closed in 1954. According to estimates, one-quarter of today's US population can trace its ancestry to someone who landed there. But immigrants began coming to the United States long before Ellis Island was established.

Castle Garden, taken sometime between 1860 to 1890. This double image is a stereograph card, which shows a three-dimensional picture when viewed through a stereoscope. *Courtesy of the Library of Congress*

The word *immigrant* first appeared in an American dictionary in 1828. The *American Dictionary of the English Language* defines an immigrant as a person who moves into a country to make it their permanent home. The word likely refers to people arriving from foreign shores *after* 1828. But many sources consider *all* people who came to the United States at *any* time immigrants, and that's the premise used throughout this book.

When many people arrive in a country during a certain period, it is called a wave. When fewer immigrants arrive, it is called a trough. Most historians agree the United States has seen four immigration waves: 1609–1775, 1830–1860, 1880–1920, and from 1965 to the present.

Irish immigrants leaving their home in County Kerry for America, 1866.
Courtesy of the Library of Congress

People relocate because of "push" and "pull" factors. **Push factors** occur in a person's native country. People might decide to leave their country because of religious or ethnic persecution; government unrest; the country's economic issues, such as unemployment; or environmental factors negatively affecting stable food sources, like the Irish Potato Famine. **Pull factors** are usually *positive* incentives propelling someone to move. Linked to the country where a person is relocating, they include improved job prospects, access to medical care or education, or a stable government. However, pull factors are not always based on facts. Rumors that streets were "paved with gold" often served as the reason people moved to the United States. Clearly that rumor was untrue.

Confronting a Growing Movement

Prior to the 1800s, many US laws dealt mainly with **naturalization**—the process to become a citizen. Before this, individual states handled immigration issues. No comprehensive and unified process existed. But as more and more people arrived, the federal government stepped in.

One of the first federal acts addressing immigrants focused on the horrible living conditions on ships. The Steerage Act of 1819 addressed conditions that delivered some immigrants to American shores in very poor health. Conditions in steerage often were so bad that diseases spread easily. Death was common. Poor diet and lack of fresh air took their toll on even the healthiest travelers.

People from steerage on deck of an ocean liner, date unknown. *Courtesy of the George Grantham Bain Collection, Library of Congress*

The act limited passenger numbers to two passengers per five tons of the ship's weight. The ship's master was fined for breaking this rule. Beginning in 1820, ships were also required to keep information on each passenger, including age, occupation, gender, country of origin, and destination. These lists of information, or **manifests**, ultimately went to the National Archives in Washington, DC, where many immigrants' records are still available and accessible today.

Although there were federal ports of entry along US borders and shores at about 70 locations, New York City served as the arrival point for 70 to 80 percent of US immigrants. But the small harbor piers were inadequate to handle the large masses of arriving immigrants. In 1847 the New York State legislature created a commission to investigate, and it reported that besides issues on the journey over, people faced many problems *after* they **disembarked** in the United States.

Pack for an Immigrant Journey

Imagine leaving home forever. That was and still is the experience for many immigrants. While people today have access to moving companies, social media, and cell phones to make relocating easier, early immigrants did not.

If you planned a trip, never expecting to see home again, what would you take? If you can't live without your cell phone, will you need to take a power source? Books might offset boredom, but they can be heavy to carry.

YOU'LL NEED

* Backpack, trash bag, suitcase, or grocery bag
* Selected items of your choice

1. Look around your bedroom or home. What items do you need for a journey? Would practical items make more sense than things with sentimental value?

2. Look at the items you feel are needed. Can your backpack hold everything? If not, what items can you do without? Think first about what items are not absolutely necessary and what items you must have. Pack everything you've picked out.

3. Set aside a "voyage" weekend when you don't have plans. Carry your belongings everywhere.

4. Can you get along with *only* those items you brought? Since food and toilets were available on steamships, you can eat at home and use the bathroom.

5. But could you survive in steerage for two weeks or more?

There was little inspection going on at the time, and no questions for immigrants to answer. Often, an immigrant's first challenge was to avoid the people at ports who wanted to take advantage of them. After all, many immigrants had little or no knowledge of the language or money in this foreign land. Other concerns were finding housing and work. Greedy landlords soon realized that increasing the number of individuals renting an apartment or room meant more money in their pockets. Often, they split up any usable space, including attics, stables, and cellars or basements, into even smaller living areas.

Boardinghouse landlords paid runners to steer immigrants to their buildings. Because runners were paid by the number of new tenants they brought, they often ran off with immigrants' luggage and belongings. Immigrants had no choice but to race behind to retrieve their items. The standard practice of these landlords was to grossly overcharge for even the most pitiful living space.

Another issue involved immigrants traveling to other states or areas. Confidence men, or con men, took advantage of people, as did **money changers**. They preyed on unsuspecting immigrants by overcharging for things like railroad tickets. In addition, some poor immigrants relied on the charity of hospitals and poorhouses for care. Dishonest individuals, who received state funds to care for sick immigrants, provided dirty and neglected conditions. With troubling reports on what awaited arriving newcomers, the New York state legislature appointed a Board of Commissioners of Emigration to find solutions to the growing problems.

In 1848 the state leased the Hubert Street pier to better control arrangements made for immigrants' housing, money, and travel. It established

STEERAGE CONDITIONS: A CHALLENGE FOR MILLIONS

Immigrants' steerage experiences depended partly on steamship companies. Some companies had higher standards for issues like cleanliness. But upon boarding, all steerage travelers made their way down narrow, steep staircases to be assigned a **berth**. There was more than one level below.

Berths were stacked two to three deep and were originally made of wood, but later of metal. Sometimes more than 100 people lived in each section. Passengers slept on straw mats with a rough blanket and received a knife, fork, spoon, tin plate, and cup for use during the voyage. Even with berths folded up to make room for tables and benches, eating in steerage would not have been the preferred choice for most people.

Once the trip was underway, seasickness was common. With bodies packed into small, poorly ventilated spaces, the smell soon became overpowering. Imagine living there for days or weeks.

Food varied and usually consisted of soup, bread and butter, cheese, stew, boiled potatoes, and stewed prunes. More than one passenger commented later about having to pick worms or bugs from the food. Passengers were responsible for washing their own dishes in large tubs of ocean water, but often passengers didn't or couldn't wash them.

Bathroom space was limited and dirty. One 1906 traveler reported five lavatories for men and two for women, for 2,200 passengers. No wonder people sometimes lived and slept in the same clothing for days with little chance for personal bathing.

In good weather, passengers found whatever space was available on deck to avoid endless days in steerage. But for millions of immigrants, their hopes and dreams rested on surviving this first voyage.

a hospital on Wards Island to protect ill arrivals. But while the situation improved for new arrivals, area residents complained about changes to their neighborhoods. They disliked the noise and disruption of so many strangers to the area. A more permanent solution was needed.

Finding a New Location

The commissioners set their sights on Castle Garden—originally called Castle Clinton, and since renamed Castle Clinton National Monument. In 1823 it was leased to the city of New York and renamed Castle Garden. During the years before Castle Garden opened, several acts passed by Congress added or changed parts of the Steerage Act. One required shipping companies to provide cooked food to all passengers. Prior to that, immigrants brought their own food. If the trip lasted longer than expected, many immigrants suffered from lack of nutrition, which led to other problems. One was a disease called typhus—referred to as "ship fever." Typhus symptoms included severe headaches, chills, and high fever. It often occurred when there was poor ventilation and sanitation combined with inadequate food. Many passengers did not survive.

But even with new laws, problems continued. The federal Carriage of Passengers Act of 1855 provided for the safety and welfare of arriving immigrants. It created guidelines that steamship companies had to follow. The act addressed items like the size and number of berths; a minimum number of ventilators; and the minimum amount of food per passenger, including how much was distributed daily. However, some requirements, such as the amount of water and certain foods required, only applied to ships leaving *from* US ports and heading to Europe, not those arriving *to* the country.

At the same time, New York passed its own law to address issues discovered by the commissioners' investigations. The city took over the vacant Castle Garden building and established one of the nation's first immigration receiving centers, which opened on August 1, 1855.

Promoting Americans and Immigrants Alike

Before ships carrying immigrants landed at the pier, they docked six miles (9.7 km) from the city. At this **quarantine** station, officers boarded to inspect for cleanliness, to report deaths, and to examine passengers and note their general health. Smaller boats took passengers to the Castle Garden pier. Sick passengers and those who required further quarantine were transported to area hospitals.

Once immigrants landed and disembarked, they entered a circular area called the Rotunda. Immigrants registered, giving their names, nationalities, former homes, and final destinations. Railroad and boat tickets could be purchased and money exchanged without worry about con men and pickpockets who confronted earlier arrivals.

One major advantage of Castle Garden involved baggage handling. A room with six bins stored items. Each bin, labeled with one letter, A

Write a Letter Home

Imagine how excited a family would be to hear from a loved one who had left for the United States. Often entire villages shared news. Some letters were even published in newspapers. How would your family feel if you moved to another country and they finally heard you safely arrived?

YOU'LL NEED

✻ Paper, lined or unlined

✻ Pencil or pen

1. Read the sidebar about steerage on page 4. Imagine what it would be like traveling that way.

2. How would you feel as you departed? How would you react when you went below deck? Do you think you'd get seasick? How would you describe the food, which might taste bad or be unfamiliar?

3. Use all five senses to share your emotions on the journey. How would the soup taste? What sounds would you hear at night? How would sleeping on a straw mat feel? What smells would fill your nose, especially after being at sea for weeks? How would you describe other passengers?

4. Write a letter to a family member describing your experience in steerage.

through F, had 600 numbers. When immigrants landed, they received a brass ticket corresponding to a letter and number from a baggage room bin. A clerk attached a similar tag to baggage and belongings. Immigrants collected baggage by giving the ticket to a clerk, who retrieved each immigrant's items from the correct bin. After the immigrant paid for handling, belongings were delivered for free to the proper train depot or steamship dock if the passengers traveled farther.

Castle Garden also offered a Letter-Writing Department to help illiterate immigrants contact relatives back home about their arrival, an Information Department for help with the next leg of a trip, and even a Labor Exchange to help immigrants find employment.

The number of arriving immigrants processed at Castle Garden between 1846 and 1855 reached 3 million, but during the years of the Civil War the number decreased to about 1.65 million immigrants. Considering that about 70 percent of all arrivals came through Castle Garden, that was still a relatively high number.

After the Civil War ended, the country expanded as an agricultural and industrial powerhouse, and foreign workers were in demand. In addition, the country's expansion into western territories provided an opportunity to settle a growing nation. Immigrants were welcomed to rebuild the war-torn country.

Southern states encouraged immigrants to locate there to work in cotton and tobacco fields, replacing workers who had been enslaved. Increased factory production in the North opened doors to immigrants too. Expansion into the West allowed many immigrants to find space where they could own land and raise families. Besides their physical contribution to the labor force, immigrants contributed to the economic well-being of their newly adopted country. By 1870 one immigration commissioner estimated that newly arrived immigrants added to the country's wealth by about $400 million each year, which would be trillions of dollars today.

The Welcome Mat Is Rolled Up

The years from Castle Garden's opening to its closing in 1890 were not without controversy. Prior to the Civil War, most immigrants came from northern and western Europe. But arrivals after the war, who came from southern and eastern Europe, were more likely to be unskilled, poorly educated, and illiterate. Many were single men who came to earn money and return home. Southern Italian men who followed seasonal **migration** jobs were called "birds of passage." Some people looked down on these immigrants, partly because they believed the newcomers were unwilling to adopt the American way of life.

In addition, resentment increased toward many immigrants—an attitude called **nativism**. In particular, those practicing the Catholic faith were resented. Some people believed that the pope, who is the spiritual leader of the Catholic Church, had secret members of his church plotting to take over the government. Certain anti-immigrant groups sprang up across the country. These organizations,

the most well-known of which was the Know-Nothing Party, pushed for limits on immigration. During this period, Congress passed many laws, including ones that excluded certain individuals from entering the United States because of mental health or other issues, or merely because they belonged to a certain ethnic group. These issues and laws will be explored in later chapters.

The Federal Government Steps In

After a fire destroyed Castle Garden in 1876, many people opposed rebuilding the immigration station. But the urgency brought on by increased immigration made it impossible to wait for a new immigration center to be created.

Unfortunately, while the building was reconstructed, old problems remained. Some people accused the commissioners of being in partnership

Treasured family heirlooms like this bible, written in Swedish and belonging to Maria Wilhelmina Lindberg Daigneau, the grandmother of the author's husband, were brought by immigrants. She came to the United States in 1891 at age eight before Ellis Island opened. *Photo by author*

Immigrants on the steerage deck of the steamer *Germanic* passing the Statue of Liberty, 1887. *Courtesy of the Library of Congress*

Could You Survive?

Life for immigrants was difficult, no matter where they settled. One of the first issues was finding a job, especially if an entire family arrived together.

Feeding a family and keeping a roof over their heads was a challenge. Expenses for fuel, food, medicine, and clothing could change from week to week. The amount of food needed increased with the number of family members. Income would be slightly higher if the mother and children worked. Photographer Lewis Hine reported that a family in the early 1900s made $1.50 to $2.00 a week altogether if a mother and several children worked every day, including Saturdays.

Planning how to balance expenses with income—the money people earn working—is called budgeting. A budget tells people how much they have to live on each week. If expenses are higher than income, families have to make choices about what they can do without.

This activity is based on one person's income in the household, from 1860 to approximately 1870. These figures are averages from different sources and will help you understand money issues immigrants faced. Prices varied depending on where a person lived and often changed from year to year.

YOU'LL NEED

* 30 3-inch-by-5-inch (7.6-cm-by-12.7-cm) index cards or pieces of paper cut to that size
* 8½-inch-by-11-inch (22-cm-by-28-cm) paper, lined or unlined
* Pencil or pen
* Calculator (optional)

1. Use the chart labeled FOOD. Write each food item and its price on one side of an index card or piece of paper. Each food item should have a separate card.

2. Turn the cards over and write FOOD on the back of each card. Set aside.

3. Use the chart labeled TOTAL DAILY WAGES. Write each day's wage amount on one side of an index card or piece of paper. Each day's wage amount should have a separate card.

4. Turn the cards over and write WAGES on the back of each one. Set aside.

5. Use the chart labeled RENT. Write each monthly rent amount on one side of an index card or piece of paper. Each monthly rent amount should have a separate card.

6. Turn the cards over and write RENT on the back. Set aside.

7. Turn all cards so only the words FOOD, WAGES, and RENT show. Keep the categories separate.

8. Pick one WAGES card.

9. To determine wages for the week, use the calculator or your brain to *multiply* daily wages by 6, since most people worked at least 6 days a week. Write that number on a sheet of paper.

10. Pick one RENT card. Using the calculator or your brain, *divide* monthly rent by 4 to determine how much is needed for rent per week.

11. Subtract that number from the total weekly wage amount. (You can check your rent and wage calculations on page 122.)

12. Now pick 6 Food cards if you live in a four-room tenement (apartment) and 10 cards if you live in a six-room tenement. Using the calculator or your brain, subtract the price of each item from the balance left after paying rent. This is the amount of money your family has available to buy *all* other items, including additional food, medicine, clothing and shoes, bedding, coal or firewood for heating and cooking, and ice for refrigeration.

13. If you don't have enough money to buy the food you need, what items would you be willing to do without?

TOTAL DAILY WAGES

Unskilled factory worker	$1.06/day
General laborer	$1.34/day
Miner	$1.46/day
Coal heaver	$1.35/day

RENT

Four-room tenement	$9.60/month
Six-room tenement	$11.80/month

FOOD

Food item(s)	Price
1 gallon syrup	$.75
1 gallon molasses	$.15
2 pounds lard	$.12
1 pound butter	$.28
2 pounds cheese	$.22
2 quarts milk	$1.12
3 pounds rice	$.27
1 pound dried apples	$.10
6 fresh peaches	$.20
8 fresh apples	$.20
1 bushel potatoes	$.59
½ dozen oranges	$.25
½ bushel corn	$.20
1 quart dry beans	$.06
20 pounds flour	$.80
3 pounds sugar	$.60
3 pounds cornmeal	$.06
3 pounds coffee	$.54
1 pound brown sugar	$.10
1 pound tea	$.16
6 pounds beef, soup	$.42
2 pounds fresh pork	$.24
2 pounds sausages	$.24
1 dozen eggs	$.26

with railroads and transportation companies and with cheating immigrants by overcharging for tickets. Still others accused the commissioners of not adequately caring for new arrivals. Grover Cleveland, governor of New York and later US president, called the handling of affairs at Castle Garden, "a scandal and a reproach to civilization."

An 1888 congressional investigation focused on the processing of immigrants at Castle Garden. Although the report never called for ending immigration or excluding people of a certain **ethnicity**, it did point out problems, including the speed with which immigrants were inspected.

After another report on Castle Garden in late 1889 noted similar problems, US treasury secretary William Windom proposed a change that would forever alter the course of immigration. In 1890 he pushed to take control of arriving immigrants away from cities and states and place it in the hands of the federal government. A Federal Bureau of Immigration was established, Castle Garden was officially closed, and the Emigration Commission in New York was eliminated.

Several new locations for an immigration station were suggested, considered, and rejected. On April 11, 1890, President Benjamin Harrison formally signed a bill naming nearby Ellis Island as the location for the first immigration station under the jurisdiction of the federal government.

Ellis Island:
A New Gateway to America

—

"The word 'America' in those days was the wish, the dream, and the hope of every person. We called that the Golden Land. It was the desire of every human being to reach the gates of the Golden Land."
—Gertrude Yellin, Russian immigrant, 1921

Ellis Island was not the first choice for an immigration station once a relocation decision was made. Bedloe's Island and Governors Island were both considered. Bedloe's Island (now called Liberty Island) serves as the location of one of the most endearing symbols of America—the Statue of Liberty. Even though the statue, a gift to the United States from France, welcomed the world's "tired and poor," many believed the arrival of those people there would damage the image of this beloved

Aerial view of Ellis Island. *Shutterstock*

gift. Nearby Governors Island was rejected because the army, which had previously used it as a military weapons, equipment, and ammunition warehouse, raised concerns.

Secretary Windom proposed Ellis Island with no objections, although the location had already been rejected. The surrounding water was too shallow for boats to navigate, and the island was too low for building projects of adequate size. Still, Ellis Island seemed the logical choice.

A Long History

Originally called Gull Island, or *Kioshk*, by the Mohegan American Indians who lived nearby, Ellis Island has had a long and colorful past. The Mohegan visited the island for the same reason the gulls, for whom it was named, did: the abundance of oyster beds surrounding it. Because of the oysters, the Dutch had named it Oyster Island.

When the British took possession of New York in the 1660s, they returned the island to its original name—Gull Island. Not much changed over the next 100 years, but the island was often referred to as Gibbet Island. That's because captured pirates were hung from gibbets, or gallows, to warn other pirates of the risks of their illegal trade.

Sometime prior to the start of the American Revolution, Samuel Ellis purchased the island. For several years, he ran a local tavern catering to fishermen. When Ellis died in 1784, the island location saw life as a concert hall, entertainment center, and aquarium. It was eventually sold to New York and then turned over to the US government in 1890.

One of the first changes to the island was increasing the land mass from 3.5 acres (1.4 ha) to about 6 acres (2.4 ha). Earth from nearby locations, as well as **ballast** from arriving ships, served as fill, after piles were driven into the shallow water. Piles are timber or steel columns driven into the ground to support vertical weight. This allowed five original buildings and seven new ones to be renovated or constructed. The new buildings included a bathhouse, main reception building, surgeons' quarters, and detention area. In addition, a deeper channel allowed access to the island along with newly built docks. The project took almost two years to complete.

Processing Improves

Construction centered on the massive three-story building. The baggage-handling room, one of the first stops for arrivals; the railroad ticket office; and a waiting room took up most of the first floor. The Registry Room, or Great Hall as it became known, filled most of the second floor. Ten aisles conducted immigrants through medical and legal procedures. The third floor—an open balcony—allowed officials to supervise activity below. Each corner of the building included a four-story tower with offices for immigration officials.

During construction, the federal government enacted the Immigration Act of 1891. Opposition to certain arrivals on American shores had grown again. This new law addressed some concerns by barring "idiots, insane persons, paupers, or . . . persons suffering from a loathsome disease, persons who have been convicted of a felony." It required shipping companies to bear the cost for **deported** individuals. This gave these companies added interest in the health of their passengers.

Three steamships arrived on the first day Ellis Island opened, January 1, 1892. That's when Annie Moore and her brothers made history. They were the first three out of a total of 700 passengers who ushered in this new era of immigration.

Tighter Restrictions Welcome New Arrivals

After Ellis Island opened, one of the first restrictions concerned not the safety of new arrivals but the safety of the US population. In 1892 a worldwide cholera outbreak caused widespread fear of immigrants. Cholera is a serious and sometimes fatal disease usually caused by bacteria contaminated water. The disease typically causes severe diarrhea and vomiting, and while it is not often

Sculpture of Annie Moore and her brothers, New York Harbor. *Courtesy of Christine M. Grote*

THE REAL ANNIE MOORE

When Annie Moore landed at Ellis Island, her name went down in history as the first immigrant to set foot there. But after the initial fanfare, including Moore's receipt of a gold coin, she faded into obscurity. So much so that her story was not only forgotten, but also recorded incorrectly.

Reports about Moore had both her age and her birthday wrong. She did not celebrate her birthday the day she stepped on Ellis Island. This information appeared in the *New York World* on January 2, 1892, reportedly based on an interview with her father. But Moore was actually 17 when she arrived, not 15 as many records indicate, and her birthday was in May.

Moore arrived on the SS *Nevada* from Queenstown (County Cork, Ireland) on December 31, 1891. She and her brothers had traveled with 145 other passengers who spent 12 days at sea. But not until 114 years after Moore made history did the truth come out. And while reports indicated she had moved to Texas, Moore never left New York and was buried in an unmarked grave just a few miles from Ellis Island.

When genealogist Megan Smolenyak dug into the story, she and New York City's commissioner of records Brian Andersson uncovered the truth. In late 1895, Moore married Joseph Augustus Schayer and lived a tough life in a tenement on the city's Lower East Side. She gave birth to at least 11 children, 5 of whom died by age 3. Moore died at age 50, and once her grave was discovered in Calvary Cemetery in Queens, New York, her descendants raised money to create a memorial to honor this notable person in immigration history.

Write a Poem to Welcome Immigrants

One of the first visions of the United States for immigrants was the Statue of Liberty in New York Harbor. American author Emma Lazarus's inspiring words from "The New Colossus" welcomed millions of them from around the world. Here is the entire poem engraved on the statue's pedestal:

The New Colossus

Not like the brazen giant of Greek fame,
With conquering limbs astride from land to land;
Here at our sea-washed, sunset gates shall stand
A mighty woman with a torch, whose flame
Is the imprisoned lightning, and her name
Mother of Exiles. From her beacon-hand
Glows world-wide welcome; her mild eyes command
The air-bridged harbor that twin cities frame.
"Keep, ancient lands, your storied pomp!" cries she
With silent lips. "Give me your tired, your poor,
Your huddled masses yearning to breathe free,
The wretched refuse of your teeming shore.
Send these, the homeless, tempest-tost to me,
I lift my lamp beside the golden door!"

Emma Lazarus, c. 1888. Courtesy of the Library of Congress

What inspiring words can you create to welcome immigrants to Ellis Island?

YOU'LL NEED

✳ Paper, lined or unlined

✳ Pencil or pen

1. Read "The New Colossus" until you get a feel for what Lazarus's words mean.

2. Page through this book and look at some of the photos of immigrants, particularly in chapters 1, 2, and 3.

3. When you think about immigration and the Statue of Liberty, what images come to mind?

4. Write a poem suitable for the Statue of Liberty's pedestal. How would you welcome "huddled masses yearning to breathe free"?

The Statue of Liberty as it stands in New York Harbor. *Courtesy of the US National Park Service*

spread from person to person, a lack of clean water and poor sewage treatment can lead to serious infection for many people. Densely packed cities like New York were especially susceptible. In previous disease outbreaks, the city had seen thousands of people die.

Although cholera victims in 1892 were mostly immigrants who had been in the United States for over two years, many cases were discovered on arriving ships. President Benjamin Harrison ordered a quarantine from September 1 until February 1893, which forced arriving immigrants to remain aboard the ship they arrived on for about 20 days before coming ashore. This allowed the illness of any sick passengers to run its course and protected the health of people in the United States. The consequences of the quarantine order were threefold. First, because of overcrowding on the ships, sickly immigrants received poor medical care, and many died. Second, steamship companies felt the pinch financially when their ships were required to keep passengers aboard for 20 days or longer before dropping them off and starting on any new voyages. Third, with the uncertainly of quarantine restrictions, immigration numbers dropped by half. This seriously affected the 50-cent tax that the US government collected on each arriving immigrant. Besides the scare of disease, an economic depression in the United States in 1893 further led to a decline in new immigrants.

The National Quarantine Act of 1893 created new health standards for immigrants, giving the federal government a stronger voice regarding

Children's roof garden at Ellis Island, 1910. *Shutterstock*

From a National Tragedy Rises a National Treasure

In the years that followed, immigrants landed in the United States by the thousands. Often, they heard "move along" or "hurry up" shouted in dozens of languages by busy employees attempting to keep lines flowing. This effort proved to be a lifesaver when fire broke out in Ellis Island's main building on the night of June 15, 1897. Since it was just before midnight, only 199 immigrants and 31 employees remained, and all managed to escape.

The building seemed to burn as easily as a pile of old newspapers. And the narrow channels around the island prevented firefighting tugboats from getting close enough to control the blaze. Crew members of a nearby paddle wheeler rescued the 55 immigrants from the hospital who were unable to move on their own. Within 17 minutes, all immigrants were safely aboard boats. Imagine the sight when the main building's roof collapsed, shooting embers into the night sky! Unfortunately, along with damage to the buildings, many state and federal immigration records dating back to 1855 were lost. Officials never determined how the fire started. But the wooden structure of the buildings was one reason the fire spread so fast.

People involved in the rebuilding would not repeat that mistake. The new structure, built of brick and iron, had steel doors. It could handle 7,000 immigrants per day, according to officials. Besides new offices for administrators and hearing rooms for special inquiries, the facility included

immigration. Another method to tighten control involved changing the questions each passenger was asked before departure. Originally, passengers answered eight questions as noted on the manifest. Another 11 were added about who had paid the passengers' fares and if passengers had ever been in prison or had depended on charity for survival. Every arrival at Ellis Island was asked the same questions. Inspectors had a copy of the ship manifests. If answers didn't match what a passenger had originally said, the passenger failed the exam. Immigrants could appeal to a **special board of inquiry**. If that was unsuccessful, they could make a final appeal to the commissioner of immigration.

new dining and shower rooms. The roof area allowed children to play games and enjoy other entertainment.

Before construction began, more landfill was brought in, increasing the island's size to 17 acres (6.9 ha). Ellis Island expanded again in 1905 and 1906, when dirt dug for the New York subway was added to create another 5 acres (2 ha). This allowed room for a contagious disease hospital. The final landfill occurred in 1934, expanding the island property to its current 27.5 acres (11.1 ha).

The Inner Workings of a Huge Complex

It takes more than an impressive building to handle immigrants. With hundreds or sometimes thousands of new arrivals every day, processing immigrants efficiently but effectively involved many people. Cooks, nurses, and custodians, along with interpreters and others, played important roles at Ellis Island. Many had been immigrants themselves.

Approximately 10 percent of newly arrived immigrants were not released after processing. Some stayed on Ellis Island for days, and others for weeks or even years. Approximately one-half of these were detained for medical reasons, and the remaining half for legal reasons. Some people dealing with health issues went immediately or eventually to the hospital, a complex of 29 buildings sitting on two manmade islands. Originally, the islands were separated by 200 feet (61 m) of water. Planners and medical staff wanted to limit the possibility of spreading infection.

Recently arrived persons at Ellis Island, 1907. *Courtesy of the Library of Congress*

Manhattan Junior Red Cross members of Public School 63 in New York City made toys at Christmas and throughout the year for sick children at Ellis Island and at the city's tuberculosis camps.
Courtesy of the Library of Congress

doctors. Even though the hospital at Ellis Island was considered a world-class facility with the best care available at the time, approximately 3,500 people died there, including approximately 1,400 children, as well as three people who died by suicide.

Until a contagious disease facility was added at Ellis Island, patients with communicable diseases were transported to city hospitals. Eventually, in addition to space for these people, the expanded building housed a maternity ward, a psychopathic ward, and a morgue. More than 350 babies were born on Ellis Island.

Officials also had to contend with one of the most basic human needs: food. While the majority of people passing though Ellis Island stayed only for hours, others remained for extended periods of time. Feeding people was a challenge because of the vastly different eating habits of people from all over the world. For example, many Irish immigrants had lived mainly on potatoes, but many Italians didn't care for the vegetable. And more than one immigrant interviewed years later thought spaghetti was really worms in blood when it was first served. Some had never seen a banana and shared stories of how they had tried to eat it with the peel on.

Dining room employees also had to contend with dietary needs based on religion. For example, one group at Ellis Island consisted of Islamic religious leaders, whose beliefs did not allow them to eat any food that the shadow of someone outside their religion had passed over. But that described *all* the food served in the crowded, chaotic dining

Children sometimes were pulled from their mothers' arms, traumatizing both parent and child. This was made worse when difficulties arose because immigrants did not understand English. Nurses often took over for mothers as they helped children recover. They were considered among the most compassionate employees immigrants interacted with at Ellis Island.

The hospital opened in early 1902 with beds for 125 patients. Two more additions brought its total capacity to 300 beds in general wards. But at the hospital's peak, often up to 500 patients stayed there at any one time under the care of about 40

Bake Italian *Mustasoles*

Mustasoles were a special treat that Italian immigrants brought with them on the voyage. Pressed into different shapes, including flowers and animals, the hard cookies kept very well on a long trip—stiff and crunchy when dry but soft and chewy after a long, damp voyage. Mustasoles have an incredibly long shelf life, and they leave no crumbs.

ADULT SUPERVISION REQUIRED

YOU'LL NEED

* 4½ cups sifted all-purpose flour
* 1½ cups melted honey, warm
* ¼ teaspoon salt
* ¼ teaspoon vanilla or lemon extract
* Bowl
* Dish towel or plastic wrap
* Cookie sheets
* Neutral cooking oil, such as safflower, corn, or soybean oil

1. Place 3 cups of flour in a bowl and add the warm honey, salt, and extract. Mix well.
2. Add enough extra flour to make a very stiff dough.
3. Knead the dough on a floured surface until smooth.
4. Place the dough in the bowl. Set aside the remaining flour for later use.
5. Cover the bowl with a dish towel or plastic wrap and let the dough rest for at least 12 hours. Do not refrigerate.
6. Divide the dough into four pieces and use extra flour to knead until smooth.
7. Shape as desired (hearts, flowers, letters, etc.) and place the cookie shapes on ungreased cookie sheets.
8. Brush the cookies lightly with oil.
9. Bake at 325°F for 15–20 minutes, until golden brown.
10. Remove the cookies from the cookie sheets while hot.
11. Let cool and allow to harden on a flat, heat-resistant surface.

room. Fortunately, after not eating for a number of days, an employee convinced the Islamic leaders that while the shadow of others might have passed over the *shells* of hard-boiled eggs, it would not have touched the inside. The men lived on hard-boiled eggs delivered with the shells on until they were released.

The Darker Side of Ellis Island

Taking care of such large numbers of people did not happen without problems. Just like at Castle Garden, vendors, clerks, and others often took advantage of immigrants. People were still sometimes overcharged for railroad tickets and swindled out of money by quick-handed inspectors.

When immigrants landed at Ellis Island, many had barely survived steerage conditions, especially in the earliest years. While the dining hall offered food for those who were detained or who otherwise chose to eat there, the immigrants had to pay for it. Another option was to buy snacks or a boxed lunch from vendors—the equivalent of ordering takeout from your favorite fast-food restaurant. Private vendors contracted with the government to provide the food. Unfortunately, just like with money changers and railroad clerks, many vendors saw an easy way to make money off the language barriers faced by immigrants. Usually the food they sold was of poor quality and overpriced. Tainted meat, apple pies made of cores and peels, and rotten fish were among the food served. Although vendors were eventually replaced, little changed regarding food quality, and immigrants were still sometimes sold spoiled food.

In the dining hall, nourishing items, such as milk and bananas, were provided on a daily basis, and many immigrants had their first taste of an American favorite—ice cream. But while the food was lower priced than food from outdoor vendors, it often lacked in quality and was priced to benefit the suppliers. For years, stewed prunes served over dried bread were fed to thousands of immigrants unfamiliar with American life.

The medical side of Ellis Island also had a somewhat somber past. While thousands of immigrants were thankful for the doctors and nurses who cared for them, and sometimes saved their

Ellis Island dining room, taken between 1910 and 1919. *Courtesy of the Statue of Liberty National Monument, US National Park Service*

lives, some practices there might seem questionable today.

Although the effects of penicillin were not discovered until 1928, scientific evidence of germs and bacteria and their spread were well documented. Cleanliness should have been of utmost importance, but on a visit to Ellis Island in 1906, President Theodore Roosevelt felt concerned enough to share his thoughts with his secretary of commerce: "The doctors made the examination with dirty hands and no pretense to clean their instruments." Fortunately, his action resulted in handwashing and sterilization practices being put into place.

Some serious medical treatments for newly arrived immigrants happened at the psychiatric ward. This 200-bed facility cared for anyone showing signs of mental health issues, such as depression, nervous breakdowns, or epilepsy. Along with immigrants, merchant seamen and Coast Guard personnel were treated there. About 25 percent of patients were immigrants, and about 10 percent of all patients treated there died.

Throughout Ellis Island's operation, immigrants with certain mental health or other conditions could immediately be deported. There was no appeal process for these unfortunate arrivals. Even people who responded to the latest treatments available had no other option but to return to their home countries. If a patient was determined to be **mandatorily excludable**, the certification by doctors was enough to warrant their return. Some diagnoses under this label included schizophrenia, homosexuality, and senility.

Many immigrants have shared positive experiences at Ellis Island, such as how they loved their first taste of an American sandwich. But as with any government or private enterprise, some workers took advantage of the immigrants' inexperience. Other workers based their judgment on information that today is considered outdated or even discriminatory.

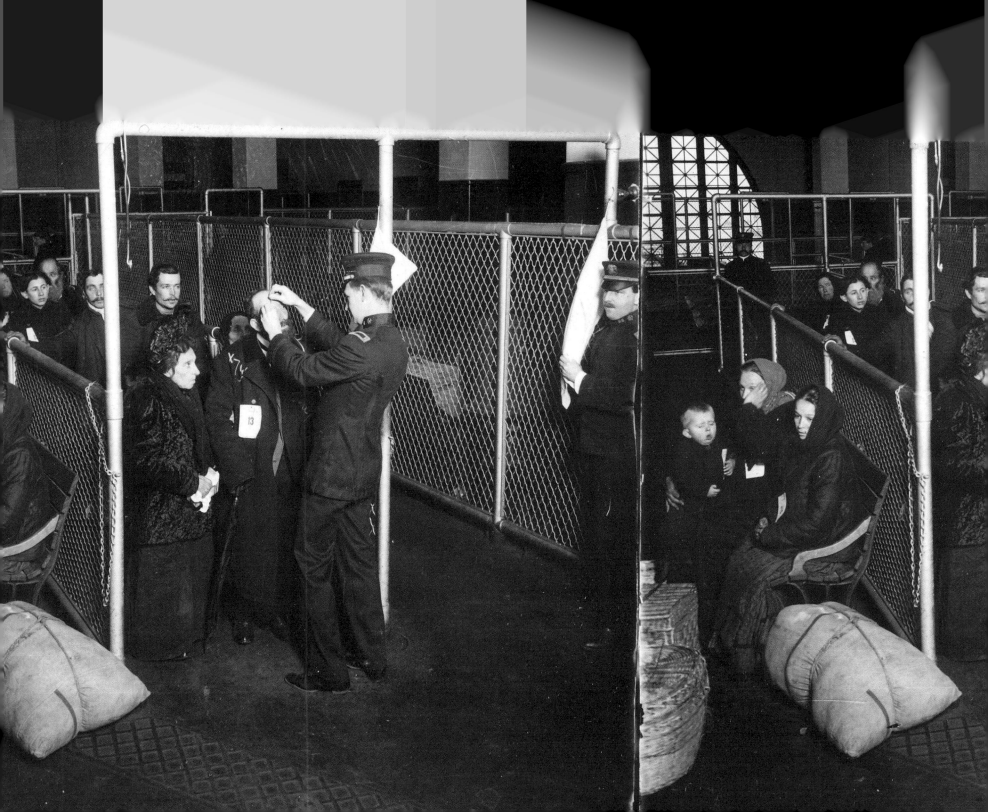

Ellis Island:
Island of Tears, Island of Joy

"Immigration officials slammed a tag on you, with your name, address, country of origin, etc. Everybody was tagged. They didn't ask you whether you spoke English or not. They took your papers and they tagged you. They checked your bag. Then they'd push you and they'd point because they didn't know whether you spoke English or not. Understaffed. Overcrowded. Jammed."

—Emmanuel "Manny" Steen, Irish immigrant, 1926

Many immigrants traveled long distances from large cities or small villages to foreign ports. Once railroads crisscrossed the world, some travelers only needed to get to the closest railway station. But many determined souls rode on donkeys or in wagons or even walked to board ships.

Inspectors examining eyes of immigrants, ca. 1900. The double image is a stereograph card, which shows a three-dimensional picture when viewed through a stereoscope. *Digital image courtesy of the Getty's Open Content Program*

Sometimes departing ships were not in port when the often travel-weary people arrived. For the approximately 90 percent of immigrants traveling in steerage, costs to get to port and to wait to **embark** only increased their travel expenses. By the early 1900s, the price of steerage tickets averaged $25 (between $870 and $970 today).

Although steerage conditions remained horrific, after 1890 most people traveled by steamship, which shortened the journey from Europe to the United States to about two weeks. US law also put more of the burden of ensuring the health of passengers on steamship companies. Before embarking, passengers were given a medical exam and then vaccinated and disinfected. This decreased **deportation** numbers because people arrived in better physical condition than previous arrivals.

Since people traveled from all over to port cities, usually many languages were spoken on one ship. Even people from the same country spoke different dialects. Imagine the excitement and anxiety, the tears and laughter, as families said goodbye knowing they might never see each other again. Italian actor and writer Luciano DeCrescenzo remembered this: "Many immigrants had brought on board balls of yarn, leaving one end of the line with someone on land. . . . After the yarn ran out, the long strips remained airborne, sustained by the wind, long after those on land and those at sea had lost sight of each other."

The Medical Experience

During peak immigration years, medical inspections of passengers before departure reduced the number of infections on board. Although passengers arrived in better health than in previous years, for many of the 12 million immigrants whose first experience in the United States started

SS *Angelo* leaving Christiana, Norway, for America, 1905. *Courtesy of the Library of Congress*

at Ellis Island, the process still played out the same. Steerage conditions were still difficult and the trip could take its toll on even the healthiest of passengers. And once they arrived, the inspection process to be admitted into the United States could still be time-consuming and frightening. First- and second-class passengers were the exception. After landing, inspectors boarded each steamship to check on the ship's condition and look for signs of disease in the passengers. New York State public health officers had the power to quarantine those who were ill with contagious diseases. After quarantine officers departed, federal officers of the US Marine Hospital Service arrived.

Passengers traveling first- or second-class were inspected in their cabins. There were few concerns about these passengers, except for issues regarding manifest information or obvious health problems. Third-class or steerage passengers went to Ellis Island for full inspection, and those with certain illnesses or disabilities were detained. At the height of immigration season, spring through fall, newcomers might wait several days to complete inspection procedures.

Upon departure, commotion added to confusion as passengers were moved along. They received a tag identifying them by their manifest number and the line number for their name on that manifest. People struggled to carry belongings and keep track of family members and children in some cases, while heading across gangplanks to one of the most overwhelming experiences of their lives. They were split into groups of 30 by each manifest. Eventually, men were separated from women and children, including boys under the age of fifteen.

The first stop was the Baggage Room, where they left most of their belongings, except for small handheld luggage they were encouraged to carry. Navigating the staircase to the second floor, people likely had no idea they were already being examined. Doctors on the upper floor watched people climb the stairs looking for breathing issues, trouble walking, or other health problems. Difficulty in climbing the stairs, especially while carrying a small item, gave doctors further indication that an immigrant might be unfit.

The Six-Second Exam

On the second floor, Registry Room staff directed passengers through aisles of iron rails leading to medical and legal examinations. By 1911 the rails were replaced by benches. Many immigrants who experienced Ellis Island remember the noise and commotion. Think about a room packed with hundreds or thousands of people speaking different languages. This was the experience of every immigrant.

Medical exams were important for the safety and well-being of other immigrants and for city and state populations, to guard against disease. Doctors became so good at identifying ailments and checking hands, faces, necks, and hair that this inspection became known as the "six-second exam." One reason for such quick exams was simply the number of people needing to be examined every day.

Any troublesome area was noted by a letter written in chalk on the person's back. Each letter represented a different medical condition. People with letters on their back were removed to special examination rooms for more thorough inspections. Doctors took note when an immigrant carried an item like a coat or shawl, which could cover up physical conditions like a missing arm or deformed hand.

People with skin diseases bathed with disinfectants before their medical exams were finalized. When you consider how long people had been on steamships with little opportunity to wash themselves, it's understandable how skin infections, rashes, and irritations occurred.

Sometimes, though, things happened that might have even amused doctors. Rachel Chenitz, who arrived from Palestine in 1920, told how her older sister had bought their mother high-heeled shoes to wear when they disembarked. Since Chenitz's mother had only worn flat-soled shoes up to this point, her walk was a bit wobbly in the heels. When doctors noticed, they examined her feet and legs. Fortunately, an interpreter helped the family convince doctors there was nothing wrong with the woman. The family eventually received permission to enter.

After 1905 the next exam involved a check for eye diseases. A doctor flipped a passenger's eyelids with his fingers or, most commonly, with a device called an eye hook, which was actually a buttonhook that women used to fasten blouses, shoes, or gloves. This exam was likely one of the most dreaded of the entire processing experience, partly because certain highly infectious diseases meant immediate deportation. Fortunately, passengers with treatable diseases were released once their infection cleared.

Doctors felt well suited to the task of identifying people with suspected mental health issues.

(top) **Women undergoing physical exams at Ellis Island, 1910.** *Courtesy of Shutterstock*

(below) **Buttonhooks like this one were used during eye exams.** *Courtesy of the Collection of Auckland Museum. Tāmaki Paenga Hira, col.2757, Wikimedia Commons*

Matching and Creating Medical Letters

Inspectors needed to work quickly, but effectively and correctly, when performing exams. Chalk letters on the backs of immigrants were recognized by every inspector and doctor. Can you determine the chalk letters used at Ellis Island? If you were a doctor there, what diseases might concern you?

YOU'LL NEED

* Paper, lined or unlined
* Pencil or pen
* Old shirt (optional)
* Chalk (optional)

1. Copy the two columns of text on the right onto a piece of paper or follow along in the book.

2. Connect each chalk letter abbreviation in the left column to the disease or medical condition that it represents in the right column by drawing a line between them.

3. Think about diseases you recognize. Ask an adult about diseases that were serious when he or she grew up. Have you heard of polio or smallpox? Not that long ago, those diseases posed a serious problem.

4. Make a list of diseases to watch for if you inspected people today. Assign each one a letter to show what problems need further inspection.

5. Don't do this part of the activity without permission. If you're using the shirt and chalk, put on the shirt or have a friend put it on. Have your friend draw a chalk letter on your back, or draw one on his or her back. Imagine the fear and confusion of not knowing what might happen to you with letters written on your back.

B	Senility
C	Heart
Ct	Physical and lungs
E	Trachoma (eye infection)
F	Lameness
Ft	Back
G	Eyes
H	Pregnancy
K	Goiter (enlarged thyroid)
L	Neck
N	Suspected mental defect
P	Hernia
Pg	Feet
Sc	Definite sign of mental defect observed
S	Scalp
X	Conjunctivitis (eye infection)
Ⓧ	Face

A list with the letters correctly matched to the conditions is on page 122.

They looked for behaviors such as nervousness, the inability to focus, and nail biting. Although doctors could decide that immigrants with certain conditions had to be deported, most deportation orders fell to special inquiry board inspectors. By 1916 a person could be deported for one or more of about 50 reasons.

Young children were not exempt from examination. Doctors particularly questioned when children who appeared old enough to walk were carried by their mothers. Doctors made children older than two walk in front of them to check for lameness. They checked whether the children could speak and hear by asking them their names.

THESE QUESTIONS COULD CHANGE AN IMMIGRANT'S LIFE

Here are the 29 questions immigrants had to answer before being admitted to the United States. Responses had to match the ship's manifest. The most important questions were numbers 6, 16, and 22, since the country didn't want people entering who would rely on government assistance. But the United States also had a law against employers promising jobs before an immigrant's arrival.

1. What is your manifest number?
2. What is your full name?
3. How old are you?
4. Are you male or female?
5. Are you married, single, widowed, or divorced?
6. What is your occupation?
7. Are you able to read and write? (yes or no)
8. What country are you from?
9. What is your race?
10. What was your last permanent place of residence? (city and country)
11. What is the name and US address of a relative from your native country?
12. What is your final destination in America? (city and state)
13. What is your number on the immigration list?
14. Do you have a ticket to your final destination? (yes or no)
15. Who paid for your passage?
16. How much money do you have?
17. Have you been to America before? If so when, where, and how long?
18. Are you meeting a relative here in America? If so, who, and what is his or her address?
19. Have you been in a prison, charity almshouse, or insane asylum?
20. Are you a polygamist?
21. Are you an anarchist?
22. Are you coming to America for a job? Where will you work and what will you do?
23. What is the condition of your health?
24. Are you deformed or crippled?
25. How tall are you?
26. What is your skin color?
27. What color are your eyes and hair?
28. Do you have any identifying marks? (scars, birthmarks, or tattoos)
29. Where were you born? (city and country)

Questions That Changed Lives Forever

After immigrants passed their medical exams, one final examination took place. This also happened in the Registry Room and might have been as scary as the medical exam. Fortunately, interpreters stood nearby to help with language issues. In front of the inspector lay the ship's manifest log with information about the immigrant before him. Each immigrant answered 29 questions and, as mentioned, answers needed to match the manifest. Immigrants knew that the fate of the next major step in their lives resided with this inspection. What many probably didn't realize was the toll these decisions took on inspectors as well. At least one inspector commented later that the constant flow of humanity sometimes pushed him to the breaking point. The weight of making decisions that affected people's lives, as well as the never-ending number of new arrivals, must surely have been difficult for even an experienced inspector.

Many questions were asked of each immigrant, and sometimes new questions were added. When Annie Moore landed in 1892, her manifest listed her name along with others and the answers to eight questions. Her legal exam at Ellis Island involved nine questions.

Although the questions were not designed to trick immigrants, one might seem that way. If you traveled to a new country, do you think that country would want you to have a job waiting? People might think having employment would be a good thing, but answering yes to that question meant

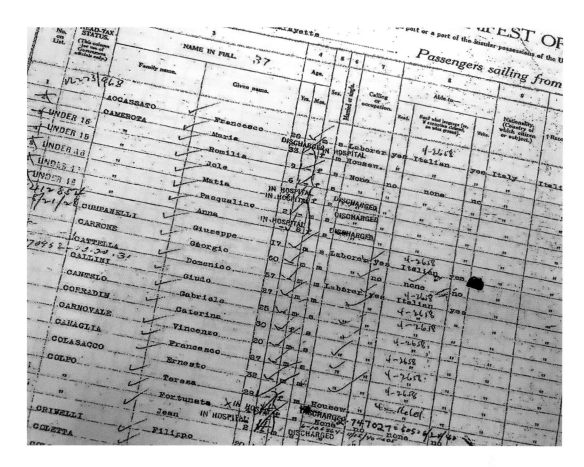

immediate deportation. That's because the federal government, and US workers and the general public, understood that many immigrants were willing to work longer hours for less pay than many American workers. In addition, companies in the 1870s and 1880s often paid for steerage tickets to bring laborers to the United States, and then took advantage of unsuspecting immigrants by paying them lower wages than promised or forcing them to work in terrible conditions. The Alien Contract Labor Law of 1885 prohibited employers from promising jobs to immigrants prior to arrival.

Copy of the ship manifest for Theresa, Jean (listed as Fortunata), and John (listed as Jean) Colpo, the author's grandmother, aunt, and uncle respectively, who arrived at Ellis Island in 1920. *Photo by author*

Children and adults at Ellis Island, 1908. *Shutterstock*

because of miscommunication about the arrival date, these immigrants were deported through no fault of their own.

Numerous stories reported immigrants receiving help from fellow passengers who had money to share or who secretly slipped them money once they finished their own inspection. Jacob Lotsky, a Ukrainian immigrant, told of his rescue by a woman he had helped earlier, on the voyage. She gave Lotsky the $25 he needed for inspection once her husband arrived to pick her up. Occasionally, inspectors approved people who were a little short on cash but who looked capable of getting a job.

The Heartbreak of Deportation

For the 2 to 3 percent of immigrants who were deported, the reality of having journeyed so far and endured so much only to be sent back to their home country must have been incredibly heartbreaking. While that percentage might seem small, a total of about 250,000 people were deported during the 62-year history of Ellis Island. Imagine selling everything you owned and sacrificing so much only to be turned away. The decision could be even more devastating if only one family member failed entry. If a child was deported, family members had to split up to return with the child, or the child returned to the home country alone. Passage home for children under age 11 and for a parent or guardian was paid by the steamship company. If a child was over 11 years old, many immigrant aid societies paid for the passage if an adult returned with the child.

One question that posed a problem for some immigrants was, "How much money do you have?" The amount required by the government varied but averaged about $25. For immigrants who made the difficult trip, passed the medical exam, and then faced that question, it must have been difficult to answer if they lacked the money. These people did not face automatic deportation. Someone could bring the necessary funds or post a **bond** on the immigrants' behalf so they could leave. Women and children, however, were never allowed to leave alone until a male friend or family member arrived for them. If no one came, perhaps

Deportation sometimes meant going back to a life of hardship, persecution, and poverty. Henry Curran, Ellis Island commissioner from 1923 to 1926, expressed his feelings when he wrote, "I was powerless. I could only watch them go. Day by day the [ferries] took them from Ellis Island back to the ships again, back to the ocean, back to what?"

A New Life Awaits

The relief at getting through the entire ordeal must have been overwhelming for immigrants. Clutching their landing card marked PASSED, it was time for them to take the final steps—exchanging money, purchasing railroad tickets (if necessary), and retrieving baggage.

Heading down the long flight of stairs, divided into three sections, was for many immigrants their last experience at Ellis Island. Passengers taking trains descended on the right; ferry riders to New York walked down the left. These stairs opened the way to new lives in the United States. But the people in the center section—the ones being detained—likely faced more uncertainty than they had when they first left their own countries. This is why many people called Ellis Island the Island of Tears, Island of Joy.

(left) **Ellis Island money exchange, ca. 1910.** *Shutterstock*

(right) **Federico and Carmela (Stanga) Pozzini, the author's grandparents, on their wedding day, December 3, 1921. Federico arrived on January 24, 1921, before quota restrictions, and Carmela arrived on November 26, 1921, after quota restrictions. Both traveled from Italy in steerage.** *Photographer unknown*

Make Your Money Count

When immigrants arrived, one process they went through involved exchanging money. New arrivals likely had their own country's money, whether it was pesos, francs, or rupees. Money exchanges changed a country's currency into American dollars.

Today there are 164 official national currencies, including the European euro, which is used by 35 countries and territories. The amount of money you get depends on the day's exchange rate—the amount that one country's currency is worth in another's.

Most exchange rates change daily, but some are fixed. *Fixed* means that a government sets its country's rate, and it does not change as often.

YOU'LL NEED

* Paper, lined or unlined
* Pencil or pen
* Ruler
* Calculator (optional)

1. Imagine you're visiting the countries your relatives came from and you plan to purchase one special item from each country.

2. Draw or photocopy Table 1 or use the table in this book.

3. Look at the list of purchases and the amount budgeted for each in US dollars.

4. Use the exchange table (Table 2) to determine how much foreign currency is needed to buy each item.

TABLE 1			
Item	Price in US $	Country	Amount of foreign currency needed
Watch	$125	Canada	156.61 CAD
Scarf	$23	Italy	
Book	$16	Tanzania	
Hat	$49	Mexico	
Chocolate	$32	Switzerland	
Painting	$75	Japan	
Shoes	$189	Bangladesh	
Jacket	$147	India	

The completed table is on page 122.

5. The US$ / 1 rate is the exchange rate you'll use when changing US dollars to foreign currency.

6. Use a calculator to multiply the price in US dollars by the correct exchange rate from Table 2. Round your foreign currency amount to two digits. The first one is done for you.

TABLE 2			
Country	**Currency**	**Currency Code**	**US $ / 1**
Canada	Canadian dollar	CAD	1.25286
Italy	European Euro	EUR	.84793
Tanzania	Tanzanian shilling	TZS	2,312.01
Mexico	Mexican peso	MXN	19.9759
Switzerland	Swiss franc	CHF	.91076
Japan	Japanese yen	JPY	110.01
Bangladesh	Bangladeshi taka	BDT	83.3145
India	Indian rupee	INR	74.0076

Based on August 7, 2021, rates

One bit of false information still repeated today is that immigrants' names were changed at Ellis Island. Name changes happened, but most likely when a shipping clerk recorded information at the port of departure. While Ellis Island inspectors verified names between passengers and ship manifests, they did not record names. In addition, inspectors and interpreters at Ellis Island usually spoke between 6 and 15 of the 170 languages spoken by the immigrants, so it is unlikely changes occurred there. Names may have been changed because of miscommunication with spelling or with pronunciation or dialect. Some immigrants may have wanted a name that sounded more "American." But there is no evidence that staff at Ellis Island intentionally changed people's names.

When It All Began

"After we had taken the oath of allegiance to the king of England, we were obliged to return to the boat.... Shortly afterwards, professional men arrived from the cities and owners of the plantations from the country who bargained with the ship's captain for our persons. We had to strip naked, so that the prospective purchasers could see that we had perfectly developed and healthy bodies. After the purchaser had made a selection, he asked: 'How much for this boy or this girl?'"

—Johann Carl Buettner, Redemptioner to Philadelphia, 1770s

Centuries before the United States existed, people were on the move. From the beginning of humankind, evidence shows that people have migrated. Two theories explain how the first Americans, as they are sometimes called, arrived. Some researchers believed people came by land and others think by sea.

The First Thanksgiving 1621, by Jean Leon Gerome Ferris, ca. 1932.
Courtesy of the Library of Congress

The First Americans: Who Were They?

One popular idea of how the first Americans arrived at what is now North America is by way of a land strait called Beringia, connecting present-day Alaska with Siberia in Russia. Ice Age climate changes caused sea levels to drop, and land masses once covered with water, such as Beringia, reappeared. But recent research has pointed to other ways these people came, mostly by way of boats from other regions of the country and world.

Unlike people who later came to America, these people were not immigrants in the strictest sense. Under the land bridge theory, they reached upper North America as hunters and gatherers who followed animals. As vast herds of animals searched for available food sources into Beringia, the first Americans followed as well.

Beringia was not actually a bridge. It was almost 1,000 miles (1,609 km) wide and did not cross over water. People lived there for thousands of years. Researchers have found remains of settlements dating back about 30,000 years. Eventually, as weather changed and glaciers melted, the Beringia land bridge gradually disappeared as sea levels rose and water covered land. People in Beringia had no way back to Asia, so they traveled farther into the continent.

Some researchers believe the earliest Americans traveled by water. Studies point to people in the Americas thousands of years before Beringia appeared. These scientists believe the length of

The painting *Short-faced Bear and Hunters* depicts early people.
© Government of Yukon / Artist George "Rinaldino" Teichmann, 2020. Courtesy of the Government of Yukon

time it took for Beringia to appear and for grass-lands to develop points to water as the way people first arrived.

Many researchers believe native people traveled along the Pacific Coast, stopping at habitable areas along the way. These people took advantage of abundant sea life to sustain themselves. Research points to movement from south to north as well as from north to south. Evidence of primitive tools—seashell fishhooks, and scrapers and hammers fashioned from rock fragments found on beaches—has been discovered in inland sites in South America. It's possible these early people then moved into North America.

These different theories are complicated by the fact that coastlines have shifted over the centuries. So researchers are even looking underwater for evidence of how the earliest immigrants came.

The Europeans Look Westward

Thousands of years after the first Americans arrived, Europeans set their sights on the New World. St. Augustine, Florida, is the oldest *continuously occupied* European settlement in the continental United States. But at the time it was established, Florida was not even part of the United States. In fact, there was no United States!

This area had originally been claimed by Spain, when Juan Ponce de León sighted the eastern coast in 1513. Some 50 years later, the Spanish king learned French Protestants had a fort there. Pedro Menéndez de Avilés landed on September 8, 1565, with approximately 500 people. He

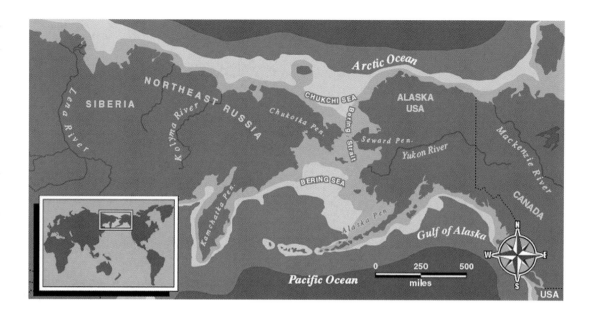

Beringia connected Eastern Russia and Alaska; the lighter color depicts Beringia land. *Courtesy of the Bering Land Bridge National Preserve*

overthrew the French and named the settlement after Saint Augustine, whose feast day was the day he sighted land.

European countries continued to send fleets to the New World. In 1585 Sir Walter Raleigh sailed with families and eventually settled on Roanoke Island in what today is North Carolina, but was then called Virginia. Two years later, Virginia Dare became the first English child born in the New World. Though Raleigh said of it, "I will live to see it an Inglishe nation," the settlement became known as the "Lost Colony" when an English ship arrived with supplies in 1590 only to find the settlement gone. Researchers still do not know what happened.

Spanish conquest extended west when a settlement was established in New Mexico in 1598. Four hundred colonists accompanied soldiers, Franciscan friars, and a group of Tlaxacalan Mexican

How Beringia Disappeared

The geography of Earth has been changing for millions of years. Ancient people once hunted, fished, and gathered food in Doggerland, which now lies beneath the North Sea in Europe. Warm inland seas once covered much of southern and western Canada and the United States. How did sea levels affect water levels and landmasses millions of years ago?

YOU'LL NEED

* Sand (about 1.5 pounds or 2 cups [0.68 kg or 0.47 L], available at craft stores)
* Large metal or plastic pan (a 9-inch-by-13-inch [23-cm-by-33-cm] pan works well)
* Water
* Measuring cup
* Ice cubes (about 50)
* Unlined paper
* Pencil or pen
* Clock or watch

1. Pour sand into the pan so that it covers most of the bottom. Leave about one-third to one-quarter of the bottom of the pan empty. Then add about ¾ cup of water until the sand is damp.

2. Pat the sand unevenly to form irregular levels.

3. Put the ice cubes in the area of the pan without sand.

4. Draw a rough sketch of your "landmass" showing how much land is exposed. Record the time.

5. Allow the pan to sit at room temperature. Check it every 30 minutes as the "glaciers" melt. Draw a rough sketch each time you check, showing how much land is exposed. Record the time.

6. When the ice is totally melted, compare your sketches. How much of your landmass ended up underwater?

If you think of your time periods—minutes or hours—as millions of years, you can understand how ice forming and melting affected Earth's land and seas and how Beringia disappeared.

Native Americans to establish ranches and instruct the local Native Americans in the Catholic faith. Spanish missionaries established a number of missions throughout the Southwest.

Because of riches in the New World, such as gold, exploration and settlement soon became private ventures that received charters from the government. A government charter, issued by a state or sovereign such as a monarchy, defines conditions under which a company operates. In 1606 England's King James granted authority to the Virginia Company of Plymouth and the Virginia Company of London to embark on voyages to establish settlements in America. The names "Plymouth" and "London" indicated what English city each company's ships departed from.

ARE SCIENTISTS CLOSER TO FINDING THE LOST COLONY?

One of the longest lasting mysteries of early settlement in North America is the Lost Colony of Roanoke. Established in August 1587, Roanoke Island had 115 settlers, including women and children.

Later in the year, Roanoke's governor returned to England for supplies, but war with Spain prevented his return for three years. When he finally did return, there was no trace of his wife, daughter, or grandchild—or any of the other settlers. The only sign that might point to what happened was a wooden post carved with the word CROATOAN.

At the time, Croatan natives lived on a nearby island now called Hatteras. There are many theories of what happened to the settlers, including the settlers getting lost at sea while trying to return to England, being killed at the hands of Spaniards from the south or by disease, or moving inland to join friendly Native Americans. However, one new theory seems promising.

Scott Dawson, a native of Hatteras, along with archaeologists from the University of Bristol, England, have uncovered tens of thousands of artifacts from a site on Hatteras. Among these discoveries are both English and Native American treasures. Swords and guns were found among numerous beads, arrowheads, and pottery. Square post holes, similar to what the English would have dug for housing, have been found not far from round post holes indicating Native dwellings. While it's unclear whether all Roanoke survivors ventured to Hatteras, Dawson believes that at least one group did, and intermingled with the Croatan, who spoke English and were helpful and welcoming of the English.

The message CROATOAN at the abandoned Roanoke colony, 1590.
Courtesy of Wikimedia Commons

The Virginia Company settlement—the Jamestown Colony—was the first permanent English colony in America. Three London Company ships landed in April 1607 in the Chesapeake Bay area of Virginia, and after establishing a governing board, they searched for a suitable location for their settlement. On May 14, the group chose an area on a narrow peninsula in the James River and built a triangular-shaped fort. The fort housed a church, a storehouse for weapons and supplies, and several homes.

The fact that there was no gold in Virginia was the least of their concerns. During the following months, the colonists suffered tragedies that almost brought them to extinction. Besides a lack of food, the colonists faced one of the worst droughts in centuries. The land was marshy and not well suited to the vegetables they planted. Also, most of the colonists were not used to hard, physical, agricultural labor. In addition, besides occasional conflicts with local Native Americans, the colonists suffered from diseases likely caused by contaminated water.

These early colonists resorted to eating shoe leather and the rats that had stowed onboard their ships and were now living in the fort. Eventually, they had to eat the cats they brought to control the rats. Researchers now have evidence that some settlers resorted to cannibalism to survive—a theory that until recently was unproven. Of the 104 original settlers who arrived, only 38 survived what became known as the "Starving Time"—the winter of 1609–1610.

Fortunately, in the spring of 1610, help arrived by way of two English ships carrying supplies and more than 150 new settlers. This aid saved these early immigrants from a fate similar to that of the Roanoke settlers. The Plymouth Company, unfortunately, was less successful. They landed in what is now Maine, also in 1607, but abandoned their settlement the following year.

Slavery's Place in Immigrant History

A discussion of immigration cannot be complete without discussing slavery. Compared to people who voluntarily immigrated—and the criminal immigrants who at least had a choice in the

Architectural remains from the Jamestown colony. *Courtesy of the Library of Congress*

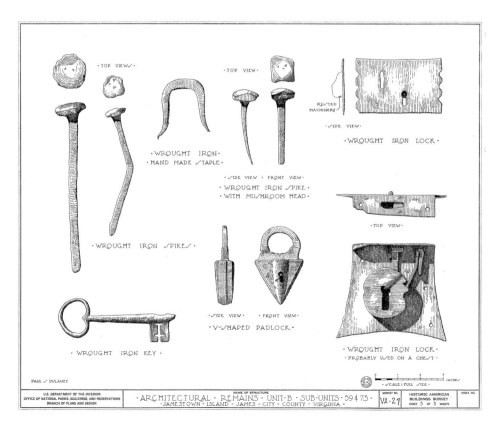

decision—enslaved people had no say. With millions of people able to trace their ancestry to the enslaved, it's important to acknowledge their place in American immigration history.

The difference, of course, between immigrants and the Black captives transported from Africa by slave traders was that the enslaved came in chains, ripped apart from their families and their lives—captives without choices. Some historians note 1619 as the year slavery first appeared in North America. That's when the first Africans arrived in Jamestown. Other scholars disagree, pointing to the enslavement of Native Americans by Spanish settlers even earlier.

Some historians believe that a settlement in eastern South Carolina in 1526 represents the first record of slavery brought to North American shores. A Spaniard from Santo Domingo, Lucas Vázquez de Ayllón, landed with approximately 100 enslaved Africans and named his colony San Miguel de Gualdape.

As happened in later settlements, the settlers struggled with disease and starvation and failed to build housing before winter. A seriously ill Ayllón, who died in October 1526, named his nephew Johan Ramirez his successor. But some settlers resisted this change. Enslaved people took advantage of this infighting and rebelled, fleeing to safety among the local Native Americans. By November, the remaining 150 settlers returned to Santo Domingo.

A little-known fact is that Africans and Native Americans sometimes intermingled. Their descendants became known as Black Indians. Some historians credit them with being the first inhabitants of the current United States to believe all people should remain free to live and thrive as equals.

A Ship Off Course Changes the Course of History

Shortly after the Plymouth and London Companies headed to the New World, another group of English immigrants attempted life in North America after an unsuccessful stay in Holland. Some members of the group applied for a charter. In return, they agreed to work for seven years and repay the money with profits made by sending goods—timber, fish, and furs—to England.

After one companion ship was unable to travel, the *Mayflower* sailed alone in September 1620. Although the original destination was the Hudson River area, near present-day New York City, the ship was blown off course during a storm. Sixty-six days after departure and with supplies dwindling, the immigrants landed at what is today Provincetown, Massachusetts. After exploring the area and engaging in minor conflicts with the Nauset, a local Native American tribe, they sailed to Plymouth.

After their initial miss of the Hudson Bay landing, the Pilgrims—as the group was called—found an abandoned Native American village along the coast. The Patuxet had died in an epidemic more than two years before, and their cleared land enabled the settlers to establish homes.

A year after they arrived, following English tradition, the Pilgrims celebrated a fall harvest in

1621, likely between September and November. Of the 102 original passengers, only 53 survived disease and starvation their first year. Those few might not have survived without the help of the local Wampanoag people, who taught them how to fish, navigate, and grow crops.

It's uncertain if the settlers would have been accepted by local tribes if they had arrived at their original destination. If not for landing at Plymouth and the kindness of the Wampanoag people, history may have been changed forever.

New Reasons to Look at the New World

Because of conflict beginning in 1618 over political and religious issues, trade in England became almost impossible. The resulting European depression affected the entire population as unemployment and taxes increased. Farmers lost their land, people were unemployed, and businesses closed. The New World looked more promising than ever.

In 1630 the Massachusetts Bay Company of England set sail with almost 2,000 people, including young families with children. This historic event began with a 17-ship fleet and opened the way for some additional 200 ships to bring 20,000 people over the next 10 years. These people were called Puritans, because they wanted to "purify" the Church of England. They favored removing any remnants of Roman Catholic rituals that remained from the origins of the church. But when the king refused to allow their ministers to preach, many Puritans found that freedom to worship was reason enough to uproot their lives.

Unlike the Pilgrims, not all Puritans favored separation from the church, but both groups cooperated with each other. However, their desire to freely practice their own faiths did not extend to others. When Puritan minister Roger Williams expressed his belief that the Puritans had stolen Native American land and argued in favor of people's rights to express religious disagreement, he was accused of spreading dangerous beliefs and banished from the colony.

In a later war with the Wampanoag, who had ensured the Pilgrims' survival, the Puritans killed their leader Metacom, also known as King Philip, and sold many Wampanoag into slavery in the West Indies.

The Dutch Move In

The Dutch began their New World influence when Henry Hudson, an English seaman, sailed for the Dutch East India Company in 1609. He traveled up the Hudson River, attempting unsuccessfully to find a route to China or India. Recognizing the opportunities for profit, Hudson encouraged establishment of a settlement in what is now Albany, New York. Little was done to bring families to the area until a charter was awarded to the Dutch West India Company in 1621. The colony of New Netherland eventually spread to most of present-day New York and New Jersey.

One community searching for religious freedom in New Netherland was composed of 23 Jewish immigrants, who fled Brazil in 1654 when Portugal took over. Unfortunately, their first

Make a Whirligig

For years, kids played jump rope, Scotch-hoppers (hopscotch), tag, hide-and-seek, and leapfrog when they weren't doing chores. They even entertained themselves while doing chores, such as by seeing who could carry the most wood or eggs without dropping any.

They also made their own toys. The whirligig is a popular toy enjoyed worldwide. Bone and clay whirligigs have even been found among Native American artifacts in the western United States.

ADULT SUPERVISION REQUIRED

YOU'LL NEED

* A large two- or four-holed button or 4-inch (10.1-cm) diameter circle made of cardboard
* Pencil or pen
* Scissors
* Ruler
* 2½ to 3 feet (8 to 9 m) of string, yarn, or heavy thread

1. If you're using the cardboard circle, mark the center, then make two small holes with scissors approximately 3/8 inch (.95 cm) from the center.

2. Thread the string, yarn, or thread through two holes of the cardboard or button. If you're using a four-hole button, thread two diagonal holes.

3. Tie the ends of the string so you have a large loop.

4. Move the button or cardboard circle until it is centered on the loop.

5. While holding the loop—one end in each hand—twirl the string in a circular motion so that it winds up.

6. Pull the string outward from both ends and then relax inward as the whirligig winds and unwinds. It might take practice to do this smoothly.

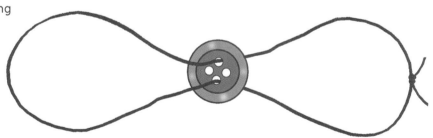

Statue of Massasoit, father of Metacom, Plymouth, Massachusetts, taken sometime between 1921 and 1930. *Courtesy of the Library of Congress*

encounter in America was not welcoming. The governor-general of New Netherland wanted to prohibit them from settling because he considered them deceitful and harmful to the colonists. But members of the Dutch East India board overruled him, allowing Jews the opportunity to settle.

William Penn also traveled to the New World because of conflicts with the English Church. In 1681 he and followers of an English religious group he founded, called the Society of Friends, or Quakers, established the colony of Pennsylvania. Penn chose the name Pennsylvania, meaning "Penn's Woods," in honor of his father. Unlike other groups that fled England because of religious persecution, the Quakers tolerated people from other countries and religions, including Jews. Penn felt so strongly about creating an ideal society that he made several trips to Europe to encourage **emigration**. In later centuries, many Germans made Pennsylvania their home.

American Colonies Become England's Dumping Ground

The founding of New World colonies was not without problems. A 1663 English parliamentary law gave courts the power to transport certain criminals there for 7 to 14 years. The law stated that "Rogues, Vagrants, and Sturdy Beggars" who went about the country "begging . . . pretending that they can tell Fortunes . . . all Juglers Tynkers Pedlers" were considered petty criminals and subject to removal. Until 1640 these "immigrants" landed in Virginia. That colony needed laborers to replace people lost to Native American attacks and to disease. But after 1640, other colonies became landing places, and most did not welcome these criminals.

In 1717 the law expanded to include felons, and the idea of penal transportation—transporting criminals to other countries or colonies—was adopted. When several states tried to pass laws denying these ships access or levying a tax on ship owners for passengers, the English king simply overruled them. Estimates indicate that over 52,000 criminals were transported to America—about 10 percent of all immigrants between 1718 and 1775, with some as young as 9 or 10 years old. When they learned they would be doing manual labor for years, but first had to survive the horrible conditions on these ships—chained to a board with a collar and padlock on their necks—some criminals chose to be hanged for their crimes instead. Those who traveled took their place in immigration history. About one-quarter of those who came died before landing, and many others arrived unable to work.

The colony of Georgia was founded in 1733 solely to provide a place for England to empty its prisons of debtors. James Edward Oglethorpe, who believed in prison reform, planned a colony allowing debtors and others to better themselves. King George happily authorized a charter since he needed people to protect South Carolina rice plantations from the Spanish. Each debtor received 50 acres (20.2 ha) of land, although he or she could not buy or sell the property.

Another system of immigration that flourished in the 1700s was that of **indentured servants** and **redemptioners**. These forms of labor were popular in southern colonies that grew labor-intensive crops like rice and tobacco. Landowners paid the servants' passage and received 50 acres (20.2 ha) of land for each arrival. The indentured servants—including men, women, and children—contracted to work without pay for a specific number of years, usually four to seven, to repay their passage.

Many redemptioners arrived from Germany. They were first given passage and then sold at public auctions to work off the debt as servants, also usually for four to seven years. Family and friends could pay off the amounts due. But new arrivals had to work off passage of any relatives who died on the voyage. Estimates indicate that almost half of all Germans arriving during the 1700s came as redemptioners.

A Great Migration Begins

"[A] crowded immigrant ship ... with fever on board—the crew sullen or brutal from very desperation or paralyzed with terror of the plague—the miserable passengers ... one-fourth, or one-third, or one-half of the entire number ... in different stages of the disease; many dying, some dead; ... the wails of children, the raving of the delirious, the cries and groans of those in mortal agony!"
—John T. Maguire, Irish immigrant to Canada, 1848

While the new colonies had a population of about 2.5 million people prior to the Revolutionary War, not all inhabitants favored independence. But when England imposed certain restrictions, many of these same people, who had begun to think of themselves as Americans, reacted with outrage.

Two of the biggest supporters of independence were themselves immigrants. Thomas Paine arrived from England only two years earlier. He worked as a journalist and wrote a pamphlet titled *Common Sense*, published in January 1776. His words convinced many colonists to fight for independence. In addition, in spite of the fact that Jews were not permitted to open retail shops, vote, hold public office, or worship in synagogues or public places, Haym Salomon, a notable Jewish immigrant who arrived from Poland in 1772, joined the Sons of Liberty. Salomon also supported the patriots financially. He gave them about $650,000, which would be millions of dollars today.

More than One Way to Win a War

While patriots stirred up support for independence, immigration to the colonies decreased dramatically during the Revolutionary War. But some Europeans who traveled to the colonies played significant roles in the war, including the Marquis de Lafayette from France and Prussian soldier Baron Friedrich Wilhelm von Steuben. An experienced soldier, von Steuben became a naturalized citizen in 1783.

The British Parliament addressed the need to increase its forces by hiring soldiers from other countries to fight. Some European rulers, such as Catherine the Great of Russia, refused to allow their countrymen to take up arms. But six small German states agreed, mainly because they needed money. These soldiers, mostly from the principality of Hesse-Kassel, became known as Hessians.

To entice these soldiers to desert, the new US government passed a law in August 1776 offering free land to any soldier fighting for England who changed his loyalty. Of the approximately 34,000 Hessians England hired, about 40 to 50 percent never returned to Germany. They either died in

An equestrian memorial in Manchester, New Hampshire, to Casimir Pulaski, a Polish immigrant who went on to become a Revolutionary War general and head of the colonial cavalry. *Courtesy of the Photographs in Carol M. Highsmith's America Project in the Carol M. Highsmith Archive, Library of Congress, Prints and Photographs Division*

battle or stayed in the newly established United States.

It's interesting to note that when the Declaration of Independence was signed into existence, eight of its signers were immigrants—Francis Lewis (Wales), Button Gwinnett and Robert Morris (England), John Witherspoon and James Wilson (Scotland), and James Smith, George Taylor, and Matthew Thornton (Ireland).

After the Patriots won independence, anyone who fought on their side gained US citizenship.

A New Look at Immigrants

In 1789 the French Revolution led to an estimated 10,000 to 25,000 new immigrants to the United States. Unlike previous immigrants, many had no intention of staying permanently. Upper-class people or royalty planned to return home once economic and political issues were resolved. Since they considered the United States a place of refuge, the word *refugee* came to describe people fleeing a country for fear of punishment for religious or political beliefs.

As the United States moved forward, the Founding Fathers considered the topic of immigration. Although they recognized the need for people to supply the growing labor force, they were still concerned about foreigners and the roles they played. But it wasn't until the Constitutional Convention of 1790 that they tackled the issue. On March 26, US delegates enacted the first naturalization law. It set a term of two years' residency for "any alien, being a free white person" to become a citizen. In addition, requirements prohibited anyone but native-born citizens from becoming president. Immigrants could, however, be elected to the House of Representatives after being a citizen for seven years, or to the Senate after nine.

Several laws over the next few years affected immigration, including one in 1795 that increased the residency requirement for citizenship to five years. The Naturalization Act of 1798 increased that number to 14 years. In the same year, the Aliens Act gave the US president the authority to arrest and imprison for up to three years any alien he felt posed a danger or threat to the nation or to remove the alien from the country. The Alien Enemies Act, passed on July 6, 1798, established that in time of war, any males 14 years or older and citizens of hostile or warring nations could be detained and even deported.

Another law, not specifically targeting immigrants, was the Sedition Act of 1798. This law made it a crime to write, print, or distribute antigovernment sentiment in any form. Because many journalists and writers were foreigners, it appeared to target immigrants. In fact, the first person arrested was Matthew Lyon, a congressman from Vermont and an Irish immigrant. He was imprisoned for writing a letter disapproving of then President John Adams.

These unpopular laws helped Thomas Jefferson win the presidential election in 1800. They were eventually repealed or allowed to expire without renewal. In 1802 Congress reinstated the residency requirement for citizenship to five years; that requirement remains today.

Immigrants Look for Opportunities

The British Passenger Act of 1803 was passed to improve conditions for immigrants. In reality, the British likely had another motive. Among the volume of people leaving England were many skilled laborers. By increasing the price of a voyage for passengers other than middle-class people, this act alone virtually wiped out the practice of indentured servants. Some laborers could not afford to travel, so these skilled laborers remained in England. Others, who simply could not afford to pay the increased price of a ticket, instead sailed to Canada and then traveled to the United States, since border laws did not exist at that time and Canadian authorities did not keep records. While immigrating through Canada meant added expense, it was still cheaper than traveling to the United States directly. This also helped them avoid having to meet inspection requirements in the US.

Over the next 50 years, immigration to the United States increased dramatically for several reasons. In 1803 the Louisiana Purchase opened an additional 828,000 square miles to settlement. With the end of the War of 1812, trade with Europe resumed. The Erie Canal construction, between 1817 and 1825, gave at least 3,000 immigrants opportunities for employment. Then, too, the Industrial Revolution significantly affected the growth of this young nation. In Europe, however, advances in machinery together with population increases created massive unemployment. So Great Britain and other countries reversed their previous rules and allowed more laborers to emigrate.

Many immigrants already in the United States created pull factors enticing their overseas family and friends to join them. Letters about life in the United States sometimes appeared in local European newspapers, and immigrants currently in the US often sent necessary funds back to their home countries for others to travel. This **chain migration**, a term used by some today, enabled hundreds, if not thousands, of immigrants to make the trip across the Atlantic.

Old Problems with New Faces

While thousands of people pinned their hopes and dreams on new lives in America, resentment against immigrants reappeared. When the number of German and Irish immigrants rose significantly in the 1820s and 1830s, so did concern about these often poor, Catholic arrivals becoming dependent on the government. But what often lurked beneath this opposition was a concern that immigrants would take jobs from Americans. Americans' reactions ranged from newspaper columns criticizing immigration to public displays of violence.

What was different about this wave of anti-immigration sentiment was that it took a much more public face. The American Republican Party, established in New York in 1843, became known as the Know-Nothing Party. The creation of this new party marked the first time the United States had a major three-party political system. Millard Fillmore, the Whig Party vice president under Zachary Taylor, who became president in 1850 when

Photographing and Videotaping Family History

Imagine finding a diary or photographs of family members who lived a hundred years ago and arrived in the United States from another country. Knowing your family's history is important. You can preserve your family's history for years to come, but you need to do it now.

YOU'LL NEED

* Family members willing to participate
* Paper, lined or unlined
* Pencil or pen
* Recording device (optional)
* Camera or cell phone (optional)
* Family photos (if available; optional)
* Photo album (optional)

1. Make a list of questions to ask your family members. Besides specific dates of births, deaths, and marriages, what other information might be interesting? Think about how family members lived, what school was like for them, what games they played, what foods they enjoyed, and other experiences.

2. Write down the information or use a recording device.

3. If you have a camera or cell phone, take pictures of current family members. Write down the date you took the photos so you'll have a record later. Perhaps an adult will help you get copies.

4. If you have family photos, get permission from a parent or other adult to write down information on the back in pencil. If you looked at the photos 20 years from now, what information would be helpful? Think about *who*, *what*, *where*, and *when* questions.

5. If you have a photo album, get permission to fill it with new or old photos. Adding "notes" to the album, like a scrapbook, will make it fun to look at later.

Taylor died, ran for president in 1856 as a Know-Nothing candidate.

The name Know-Nothing came about because the party's members were banned from sharing details. If nonmembers asked about the organization, the party member explained what he supposedly knew . . . nothing. The Know-Nothings pushed to have Catholics and foreign-born people removed or banned from holding anything but minor public offices, to require Bible reading in schools, and to institute a 21-year requirement for naturalization.

Irish families weren't their only targets. Anti-immigrant rallies, which often turned violent and deadly, targeted other ethnic groups, including German, Hungarian, and Polish natives. The Know-Nothing Party also wanted to forbid the people they deemed unfit—lunatics; criminals; and people who were blind, destitute, or insane—from entering the United States. After the development of the modern Republican Party in 1854, the Know-Nothing Party fell out of power by the late 1850s. While many former Know-Nothings joined the newly created Republican Party, nativism still exists today.

The Great Hunger Strikes

During the 1820s and 1830s, almost 145,000 immigrants came to the United States from Ireland, Germany, England, Scotland, and France. In the next decade, the number skyrocketed to almost 600,000.

Push factors often played greater roles in promoting immigration. One of the most well-known of those involved a vegetable that originally made it to Europe *from* the New World—from what is now Peru in South America. That tuber is the lowly potato.

In Europe, the years before the Irish Potato Famine were prosperous for many people, and there were many dramatic population increases. Ireland, already one of the poorest countries in Europe, was among those countries that saw its

Memorial to the children of the Great Hunger, County Clare, Ireland.
Courtesy of Mikala Pritts

population grow. The population in 1791 increased about 70 percent in 50 years, and Ireland became the most densely populated country in Europe.

Because the country had faced blights (plant diseases that destroy crops) before, people took the problem in stride when a blight was reported in 1845. But a new strain of disease had traveled from the United States to Europe. While other countries also saw this new blight invade their farmlands, it affected Ireland more because Irish people relied almost solely on potatoes for their diet. It's estimated that about one-third to one-half of the entire Irish population at the time—about 3 to 4.5 million people—ate little else.

During the 1846 blight, certain parts of Ireland lost their entire potato crop. When the situation worsened in 1847, many people couldn't pay their rent. Most tenant farms were owned by Irish and English landlords. But the Irish Poor Law Extension Act, signed in 1847, required Irish landlords to support the poor. Britain blamed farm mismanagement on the landlords and did little to help. As the famine continued, landlords found themselves strapped for cash and, ultimately, about half a million people were uprooted from their homes. Emigration was an increasingly popular option.

The loss of adequate housing and food, a lack of proper hygiene, and an increase in lice and other pests caused widespread outbreaks of disease in the Irish people, including a strain of typhus called famine fever. Although more Irish people in Ireland died from disease than from lack of nutritional food, about 1 to 1.5 million deaths were from starvation due to the famine.

TWO NATIONS UNITED IN TRAGEDY

Few victims of the Great Hunger could have expected help from people who themselves had a history of tragedy. But the Choctaw nation, now in Oklahoma, drew on their own experiences to alleviate Irish suffering.

Only 15 years before, the Choctaw nation, along with thousands of other Native Americans, were sent on deadly forced marches from their homelands in the Southeast to lands west of the Mississippi. The US National Park Service estimated that approximately 100,000 Native Americans were uprooted to make way for White settlement. Thousands of people died from exhaustion, exposure, and starvation during the more than 1,000-mile march.

In 1847 the Choctaw people, still struggling after their forced relocation, raised $170 (over $5,000 today) for Irish relief. Tribal council leader Delton Cox said the people gave an outpouring of support because they remembered their own hardships, though they themselves were poor.

In gratitude, the Irish commissioned a sculpture, appropriately named *Kindred Spirits* and dedicated in 2017 in Middleton, County Cork. Choctaw nation chief Gary Batton, along with other members of the tribal delegation, attended the unveiling of the sculpture.

In 2020, the Irish people remembered the generosity of the Choctaw people by supporting them in a modern tragedy—the COVID-19 pandemic. Native Americans are often hardest hit during disease outbreaks, because of factors such as poverty and lack of basic necessities like running water. As of

October 2020, over 20,000 Irish donors had contributed more than $1 million to the Navajo and Hopi Families COVID-19 Relief Fund. The Choctaw have a word for this—*iyyikowa*—which means "serving those in need."

Kindred Spirits sculpture honoring the aid of the Choctaw nation, Middleton, County Cork, Ireland. *Courtesy of Alex Pentek. Kindred Spirits. 2015. (Image: Red Power Media)*

Historians today disagree about the issues contributing to the Great Hunger, as it was called. But this tragedy changed the course of history and increased the number of people leaving Ireland. Unfortunately, many who managed to purchase tickets *for* travel were not necessarily in good enough health *to* travel. Thousands of Irish immigrants traveling to the United States by ship faced inhumane conditions, including a lack of ventilation, onboard medical personnel, sufficient food supplies, and clean water. About 20 percent of all Irish passengers died on these so-called coffin ships. Many others arrived in the United States in horrible condition.

The Rush for Gold

While some people looked across the Atlantic Ocean for a new life, others looked across the Pacific. The pull on the West Coast was similar to the claim that US streets were paved with gold. But this pull was *Gam Saan*, Chinese for "gold mountain." When gold was discovered at Sutter's Mill on January 24, 1848, the mill's owner, John August Sutter, hoped to keep it secret. But news like this doesn't stay quiet for long, and word soon traveled not just across the United States, but also across the world.

Initially, many people thought the gold discovery was a hoax. But soon gold fever took hold. Among those who rushed to California to make their fortune was the first large group of Chinese immigrants. Before the gold rush, Chinese arrivals were considered hardworking and industrious, but some people's attitude toward Chinese natives quickly changed.

One issue involved the willingness of Chinese miners to work areas abandoned by other forty-niners, as miners were called (because the gold rush began in 1849). The Chinese miners often worked an area for every last speck of gold.

White miners felt Chinese miners found gold that belonged to others. Among those harboring

James Marshall, discoverer of gold at Sutter's Mill, ca. 1850. *Courtesy of the Library of Congress*

Panning for Gold

Gold has been a prized possession throughout history, to make objects and jewelry and as currency worldwide. For thousands of immigrants, the possibility of discovering gold was the pull factor that brought them to the United States.

   Although gold is not found everywhere, certain areas, especially where land has been formed by glaciers, are good places to start looking. If you live in an area not known for gold discoveries or if you don't have access to a natural stream or creek, you can still have fun dry panning for gold in your backyard. Gold is often found as flakes, pickers, or nuggets. A flake—or fleck—is any piece of gold you have to wet your finger to pick up, and a picker is a piece you can pick up without wetting your finger. And a nugget? You'll know it when you see it!

ADULT SUPERVISION REQUIRED

YOU'LL NEED

* Metal pie pan
* Small shovel or trowel
* Small bucket with water (needed for dry panning)
* A good location, preferably a shallow stream

1. Before you start, be sure you're in a location where you're allowed. Don't pan on private property without permission. Local, state, and national parks might have rules about panning, so check first.

2. If you're panning in a stream, the best place to start is where there are small rapids or a bend in the stream. Gold is heavier than rocks or other similar sized items, so as water flows, the gold will drop.

3. Fill your pan with a scoop of dirt and gravel from the stream. Pick out any large rocks.

4. Add water so the dirt and rocks are well covered.

5. With two hands, move the pan in a circular motion and allow the water to spill over the sides. This washes the dirt off the rocks and allows small stones to flow out with the water.

6. When most of the water is gone, carefully tilt the pan to drain off excess water.

7. Add more water and gravel. Continue washing the gravel and rocks with circular motions.

8. When you have mostly sand left, carefully move the remaining sediment around with your hands to look for gold. The first try is called the test pan.

9. Good luck!

An authentic gold pan showing nuggets and pickers. *Courtesy of Gloria Adams*

A modern-day gold panner teaches his grandson how to pan for gold.
Courtesy of Gloria Adams

anti-Chinese attitudes were German and Irish miners, some of whom had themselves faced discrimination elsewhere. California addressed the situation by enacting the Foreign Miners' License Act in 1850, requiring non–US citizen miners to pay a $20-a-month license for permission to mine. This act was principally aimed at Chinese, Latin American, and Mexican miners.

At the time, the California territory belonged to Mexico and had fewer than 1,000 non–Native American residents. But soon after gold was discovered, the Treaty of Guadalupe Hidalgo was signed on February 2, 1848, ending the Mexican-American War. The treaty gave parts or all of a number of western states, including California, to the United States. Mexican citizens could stay in the new territory or return to Mexico; about 3,000 returned home.

Those staying could become US citizens, or remain Mexican citizens with all the property rights given to US citizens under the Constitution. But the Foreign Miners' License Act also required these people—called Californios—to pay the monthly fee. These new citizens, referred to by the derogatory term *greasers*, were often denied rights outlined in the treaty. California even adopted the Anti-Vagrancy Act of 1855, also known as the Greaser Law. This law allowed for the arrest and imprisonment of vagrants: low-wage earners or unemployed people considered "idle," who sometimes begged for food or money and were seen as nuisances. Most of these people were Mexicans, Californios, Native Americans, and Asians. New Mexico, which qualified as a state soon after its annexation from Mexico, did not achieve statehood until 1912 because many looked on its citizens as not "American" enough.

Immigrants who came from as far away as Europe made up about one-third of the total number of miners, but the Chinese made up the largest non-White group. In 1851 just under 3,000 Chinese immigrants arrived; that number spiked to 20,000 in 1852 alone. Although the miners' law was repealed in 1851, it was reenacted in 1852 and again targeted Asians.

The fee was reduced to three dollars a month, but particularly for Asians, who earned an average of six dollars a month, the fee was enormous. And while the three-dollar monthly fee may seem small for others earning more, demand for food, tools, and clothing had risen dramatically during the gold rush, along with prices. One egg cost about $1 in 1850, which equals around $33 today.

In addition, riots sprung up and many Chinese were physically abused, accused of crimes they did not commit, or even murdered.

The only people treated worse were Native Americans. Hundreds were abused or enslaved by Sutter and others. The law even allowed people to take orphaned Native American children and enslave them until age 18. Because of the government's position after California became a state, between 9,000 and 12,000 indigenous people are believed to have been murdered by government militia, settlers, and others. From the beginning of the gold rush until about 1870, the Native American population in California fell from approximately 300,000 to about 30,000 due to violence and diseases, including measles. When you consider that these people trace their ancestry back thousands of years, these first Americans faced some of the worst discrimination ever.

R.114467.   A 11167.

114467

154. ²⁶⁵ (7)

Dan. Hi. Loy.
Sierra City
37 years 5 ft. 5¼
Cook
Sierra City
no marks.

R.114465.   A 11165.

114465

152.

Noy
Sier
changed
from L
Noy. H
32 yea
min
no

114466.

R.114466.   A 11166. 
153. ¹⁷¹ (6). Cook
Chin Hung
Forest City
Jin Hung changed to
Chin Hung by interpreter
54 years   5 ft. 2"
Forest City
second finger of right
hand very short.

114464.

R.114464. 
151.
Lock
63 years.
miner
San. Jo
no m

De

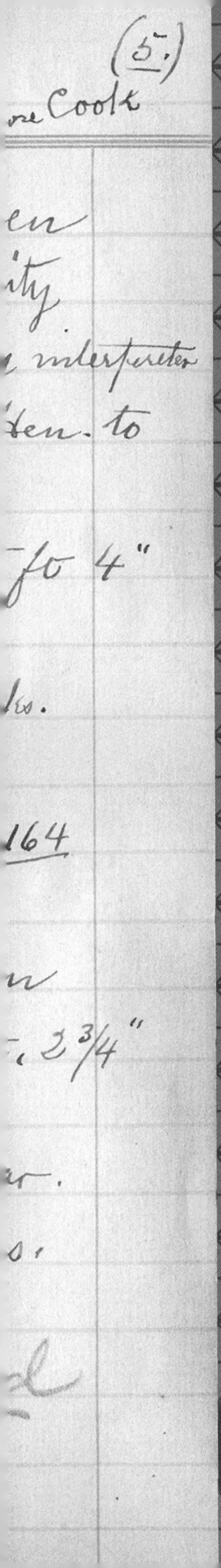

6

A New Country Confronts New Changes

—

"It was a beautiful morning, and as I looked over the rail … my hopes rose high that somewhere in this teeming hive there would be a place for me. What kind of place I had myself no notion of. I would let that work out as it could. … I had a pair of strong hands, and stubbornness enough to do for two; also a strong belief that in a free country, free from the dominion of custom, of caste, as well as of men, things would somehow come right in the end, and a man gets shaken into the corner where he belonged if he took a hand up in the game."

—Jacob Riis, Danish immigrant, New York, 1870

With the start of the Civil War, immigration hit a new low, as did discrimination against immigrants. The need for soldiers and several acts passed by Congress during the war significantly affected immigration for years to come.

This notebook showing Dan Hi Loy, cook; Chin Hung, cook; Noy Hen, miner; and Lock Yan, miner, was kept by a Sierra County, California, justice of the peace to enforce anti-Chinese laws, taken sometime between 1890 and 1930. *California Historical Society*

Men claiming exemption from the Civil War draft, 1863. *Courtesy of the Library of Congress*

The federal government increased the number of Union troops by offering bonuses of several hundred dollars to new recruits. Immigrants were guaranteed citizenship after discharge. The government denied actively promoting immigration in exchange for increasing Union troops, but recruiting tents were set up near Castle Garden.

New Arrivals Take a Stand

Many immigrants rushed to defend their new country on both sides. Immigrants' views were based less on ethnicity and more on geography. Those in the North supported the Union, and those in the South supported the Confederates. More than 540,000 immigrants served during the war, even some who didn't speak English and had only recently arrived. Entire regiments, such as the First German Rifles, the Spanish Guard of Mobile, and the Irish Brigade, formed on both sides.

Immigrants were also swayed to enlist by the Homestead Act of 1862. It awarded up to 160 acres (64.7 ha) of public land to any adult heads of households or to those over 21 years old who were US citizens or had shown intent to become citizens. Homesteaders were required to live on the land for at least five years, pay a filing fee, make improvements, and plant at least 10 acres (4 ha). The residency requirement could be shortened by six months by paying $1.25 per acre for 160 acres (65 ha) or $2.50 per acre for 80 acres (32.4 ha) or less. In 1864 the homestead residency requirement for former Union army members was lowered to one year.

To fill their rosters, Confederates crafted the first draft act in April 1862, requiring White men ages 18 to 35 to register to serve, except those involved in businesses crucial to the war effort or the benefit of society. Plantation owners with more than 20 enslaved workers were also exempt from the draft.

District **quotas** set the number of recruits in the South. If not enough men joined the Confederate army, a lottery chose others to serve. One controversial provision gave drafted men the option to hire someone to fight in their place or pay a commutation fee to avoid that round of the draft. This raised the notion that this was "a rich man's war and a poor man's fight." Because African Americans were not considered citizens, they were exempt from the draft.

The Union Army responded with the Civil War Military Draft Act, signed by President Abraham Lincoln on March 3, 1863. Referred to as the Enrollment or Conscription Act, it affected US citizens or immigrants who had applied for citizenship who were ages 20 to 45, and unmarried men ages 35 to 45. Many immigrants opposed abolishing slavery and felt singled out, since paying a fee to avoid service was not an option. This raised the rich man–poor man's argument. Some Irish immigrants feared job competition from formerly enslaved people. Democratic Party members and antiabolition or antiwar newspapers promoted this idea. Britain openly supported the South, fueling long-held resentment among Irishmen, who still blamed Britain for its failure during the potato famine.

On July 13, 1863, less than 48 hours after the first New York draft lottery, mayhem broke out. Initially directing their anger at African Americans, rioters turned to Republican Party supporters or businesses owned by them. Called the bloodiest rioting in US history by some historians, over 100 people died in the New York City Draft Riots, including 11 African American men who were lynched. The four-day riot ended when a New York regiment arrived from Gettysburg, Pennsylvania, and assisted the police. When the draft lottery resumed in August, there were no public displays of opposition.

President Lincoln, who had issued the Emancipation Proclamation, pushed for the country's only act to promote immigration. An Act to Encourage Immigration, signed into law on July 4, 1864, allowed immigrants to pledge up to one year's wages in return for passage. The signed contract required repayment of the money, just like indentured servants before. But when thousands of military members returned after the war looking for jobs, finding employment and repaying money for passage became more difficult. The act fell to repeal in 1868.

The West Pulls Again

While the North and South fought, the federal government approved a construction project that forever united the East with the West. But the Transcontinental Railroad project had its own problems.

The Pacific Railroad Act, signed in 1862, gave two railroad companies the authority to lay almost

Draft rioters burning and sacking the Colored Orphan Asylum in New York City, 1863. *Courtesy of the Library of Congress*

1,800 miles (2,897 km) of track, including through the steep and rugged Sierra Nevada Mountains. In 1863 the Central Pacific Railroad began construction eastward from Sacramento, California. The Union Pacific Railroad began construction in 1865 westward from Council Bluffs, Iowa. But because of the war, there weren't enough male workers for this monumental building project. And with ethnic discrimination during the gold rush still fresh, history was preparing to repeat itself.

As the war dragged on, the Union Pacific laid only 40 miles (64.3 km) of track from 1863 to 1865. Many workers were Irish, but Swedes, Danes, and freed African Americans also worked on the railroad. When the Central Pacific began construction, it had fewer than 800 workers for the work of about 4,000 laborers. The Central Pacific turned to the numerous Chinese laborers who had arrived looking for gold.

The completion of the Transcontinental Railroad, May 10, 1869. *Courtesy of the Library of Congress*

Originally, the Central Pacific hired only 50 Chinese workers, because officials were skeptical about these men being able to handle the back-breaking task. When the first crew proved more than capable, more were hired. Ultimately, about 12,000 Chinese workers, out of about 14,000 laborers, found employment.

Despite their work ethic, Chinese workers received less pay than White workers—up to 30 to 50 percent less. White workers received food and shelter; Chinese workers supplied meals and tents at their own expense. Chinese workers were assigned the most difficult tasks, and about 1,000 died during construction. The railroad was completed on May 10, 1869, when a ceremonial golden spike was driven into the rails at Promontory Summit, Utah.

When the Fourteenth Amendment was added to the Constitution on July 9, 1868, it stipulated that "all persons born or naturalized in the United States, and subject to the jurisdiction thereof, are citizens of the United States and of the state wherein they reside." This specifically referred to African Americans and enslaved people who were emancipated, or freed, after the Civil War. Children of immigrants qualified as well.

Chinese Face Federal Discrimination

The first federal law targeting an ethnic group was enacted on May 3, 1875. The Page Act specifically addressed Chinese women emigrating for "immoral purposes" and laborers and convicted felons from China, Japan, and other Asian countries. Many of the problems California and its cities faced were blamed on these people. Backlash included forbidding Chinese children from attending public schools; requiring fees from laundries, most of which were run by Chinese people; and cutting off the braids of convicted Chinese men as an act of humiliation. Labor unions opposed allowing the Chinese to join.

In 1879 California passed laws to restrict the Chinese from working public jobs and voting and to punish companies that imported Chinese workers. But, despite discrimination, the number of Chinese people immigrating between 1880 and 1881 doubled, and it more than tripled in 1882 to almost 40,000. The federal government stepped in to address hostility, but not how you might think. The Chinese Exclusion Act, passed in 1882, banned Chinese immigrants for a period of 10 years; later amendments kept those who left the United States from returning. The original act, expanded in 1892, also required the Chinese to carry an identification certificate at all times. Individuals caught without one were deported. But getting the certificate required a Chinese worker to be fingerprinted and have at least one White witness vouch for him or her. Even people born in the United States, or who had parents or spouses who were American citizens, had trouble getting the paperwork. When the law was challenged to the Supreme Court, the government prevailed.

Only Chinese laborers were named in the act; merchants, teachers, clergy, and others were excluded. Since anyone born in the United States was a citizen, the children of Chinese citizens could enter. Some men and a few women brought

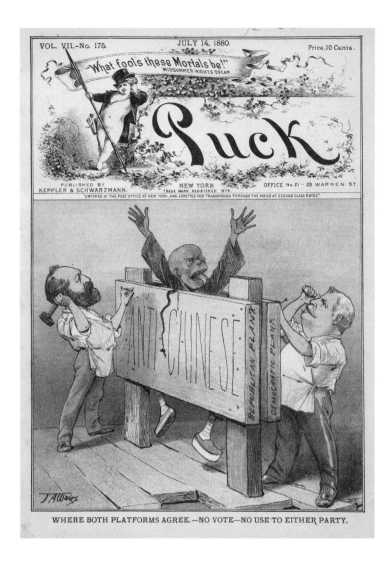

WHERE BOTH PLATFORMS AGREE.—NO VOTE—NO USE TO EITHER PARTY.

Anti-Chinese cover, *Puck* magazine, 1879. *Courtesy of the Library of Congress*

papers proving they were sons or daughters of Chinese US citizens. These so-called **paper sons** and **paper daughters** increased the number of Chinese immigrants, particularly in the West.

Japanese immigrants also faced discrimination. Many of them, mostly men, found work instead in Hawaii, which at the time was a sovereign country. But work on sugarcane plantations

Create a Topographical Map

Without immigrants, the Transcontinental Railroad might not have been built. But when construction began, builders first needed to know the landscape ahead. Information about rivers, mountains, and forests helped surveyors map out areas to lay track. It helped builders prepare for ways to go around, over, or through obstacles.

One way to depict land formations, waterways, roads, and vegetation is with contour or topographical maps. Topography is the study of land surfaces, both natural and manmade. Topographical maps show the depths of bodies of water and the height of hills and mountains. Surveyors use accurate tools for taking measurements, which today include satellite imagery or remote sensing equipment.

YOU'LL NEED

* ¼-inch (.64-cm) thick carboard pieces, varying sizes, with at least one 8-inch-by-8-inch (20.3-cm-by-20.3-cm) or larger piece
* Pencil or pen
* Scissors
* Colored markers, pencils, or crayons
* Glue
* Graph paper, one sheet
* Calculator (optional)

1. Use the large piece of cardboard as the base for your map.

2. Draw four to five irregular shapes on pieces of cardboard for mountains, all different shapes and sizes. (See the illustration on page 65.)

3. Cut out the shapes. Cardboard can be hard to cut, so get help if needed.

4. Color the edges of these shapes brown, the color used on topographical maps to show elevations.

5. Glue the cut cardboard pieces on top of each other from largest to smallest, but don't glue them to your base.

6. Set your mountain on the graph paper, but don't glue it.

7. Decide how many feet each square on the graph paper represents. The map key could equal 10, 25, 100, or some other number of feet per square. Write this key on the graph paper. For example: ¼ inch (6.4 mm) = 200 feet (61 m).

   Mark the width and length of your mountain's edge on the graph paper and then count the number of squares between those marks. You will have two numbers—width and length.

8. Use the calculator or your brain to multiply the number of squares for length and width by the feet from your map key. That's how long and wide the base of your mountain is in feet. This is just an estimate, but if you used real equipment your measurements would be exact.

9. Count the elevations—the layers of cardboard you used—on your mountain.

10. Multiply the number of elevations by the number of feet from your map key to determine how tall your mountain is.

11. Remove the graph paper and glue the mountain anywhere on the base.

12. Draw roads, rivers, or vegetation.

13. Color the map and the layers of the mountain. On topographical maps, rivers and waterways are blue, highways are red, vegetation is green, and unpaved roads are orange.

14. Congratulations! You've made a topographical map.

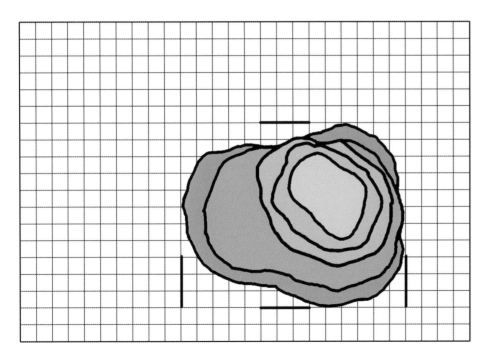

Topographical map

was as grueling as that in mines and on railroads. In 1906 Congress passed a law excluding Japanese immigrants as well.

Another law, the Naturalization Act of 1906, allowed the government to remove naturalization from people found guilty of becoming a citizen through fraud, such as making false statements or from people who lacked good moral character. This also applied to women who married foreigners, although it did not apply to men who did the same. The law was repealed in 1940.

Resentment Grows as Immigration Numbers Expand

As railroads expanded throughout the country, so did the need for workers. With Chinese workers excluded, Mexicans stepped up to fill a hungry industry. Railroads offered Mexicans six-month contracts to lay track. But Mexicans faced their share of discrimination, just like others had.

Again, anti-immigration supporters put pressure on Congress to respond. Congress enacted another more expansive law—the Immigration Act of 1882. This law specified a number of undesirables, including anyone likely to become a public charge—people who might have difficulty finding or keeping a job and who might need to rely on the government for support. This became a guiding principle in immigration legislation for years. In addition, the 1882 law required a head tax from every non-US citizen arriving on American shores from a foreign port. While the official reason was

to offset the cost of immigration services, the tax also prevented poorer people from entering.

Feelings of nativism combined with beliefs that immigrants threatened the country's stability. Many people viewed them as **anarchists**, individuals who rebelled against authority, espe-

---

EUGENICS

Eugenics gained public support in the late 1800s. The idea that human beings could be perfected affected immigration laws throughout history, beginning with the Immigration Act of 1891, which prohibited "idiots" from entering the United States. Even **segregation** and marriage laws were enacted to prevent certain defects from somehow infecting the White American race that many people favored.

Anti-immigration groups used this theory to prevent immigrants from entering based on the belief that certain ethnicities would pollute the US population. Howard Knox, a leading expert on mental testing who worked at Ellis Island, believed one immigrant could adversely affect generations to come as defects, such as feeble-mindedness, or below-average intelligence, were passed on through children.

One immigrant selected by a team of scientists studying eugenics at Ellis Island was classified as having low intelligence, partly because of the shape of his head. When the man was later tested, the Knox team found that the man, who spoke three languages, tested above average.

In 1923 the American Eugenics Society was created. But the notion of eugenics died out after World War II, when reports of the cruel experiments that Nazi doctors performed on Jews and others deemed unworthy became known. Hitler's attempts to create a superior race were based on eugenics.

As genetic testing continues to advance, some people still share concerns about the push for a superior race to weed out human characteristics that are considered negative.

---

cially established governments. On May 4, 1886, in Haymarket Square in Chicago, an anarchist group held an initially peaceful protest against police brutality and supporting workers' rights that attracted national attention. But it wasn't the rights of immigrants and working-class laborers that made this event historic. An unidentified individual threw a bomb that exploded during the protest, killing one officer, and police fired on the crowd. A riot resulted in the deaths of 17 people. This event affected anti-immigration attitudes and legislation for years. In 1901, after the assassination of President William McKinley by an unemployed anarchist, being an anarchist was added as an excludable offense for entry into the United States.

Despite these negative views, many middle- and upper-class Americans had never had direct contact with immigrants. Newspaper cartoons, often racist, were their only connection. Some cartoons portrayed Jews with hook noses, Irishmen as apes, and Chinese as locusts or worse. But two photojournalists, Jacob Riis and Lewis Hine, took an active role in bringing the plight of immigrants to the attention of average Americans.

Riis, himself an immigrant, began taking photos as a police reporter. Often finding himself in the poorest, most crime-ridden areas, he wrote a book, *How the Other Half Lives*, that helped bring about much needed housing reform. President Roosevelt felt so strongly about Riis's work that he called him "New York's most useful citizen."

Hine took an interest in documenting immigrant stories after becoming a school photographer in New York. He traveled to Ellis Island and the Deep South to photograph children working in harsh conditions. His photos helped reform child labor laws.

Riis and Hine showcased the difficulties of immigrant life—overcrowding, poverty, hunger. Because of their work, many Americans saw the reality of immigrant life for the first time.

After Ellis Island opened, an increase in the number of Europeans from eastern and southern countries fueled a growing movement to restrict or limit newcomers. At the beginning of the 1890s, about 956,000 immigrants arrived from these countries, compared to approximately 3.8 million immigrants from northern and western European countries. By the end of the 1890s and into the 1900s, immigrants from eastern and southern European countries outnumbered northern and western immigrants by over 1.5 million.

One of the United States' most outspoken and long-lasting anti-immigration organizations was the Immigration Restriction League, established in 1894. The founders were especially concerned about the newest wave of immigrants—particularly Catholics and Jews, again from southern and eastern European countries. Anti-immigrant sentiment surged after a report showed a dramatic increase in immigrant populations in large cities. It was predicted that these populations might grow to almost 80 percent of the total people living there. Again, fear grew that American jobs would be lost to these "undesirables."

While immigration continued, so did the number of people who traveled to Canada on their way

(above) **Lewis Hine, self-portrait, ca. 1930.** *Gift of the Photo League, New York; ex-collection Lewis Wickes Hine, Wikimedia Commons*

(left) **A rear tenement bedroom, New York's East Side, 1910.** *Photo by Lewis Hine, Digital image courtesy of the Getty's Open Content Program*

to the United States. One reason was the increase in requirements at ports like Ellis Island. Steamship companies, which had previously advertised the comforts and conveniences of traveling on their lines, promoted travel to Canada, which was usually cheaper.

Eventually, the US government contracted with Canadian steamship and railroad companies in 1894 to regulate immigration. Steamship companies agreed to complete ship manifests and bar

Stow Away a Time Capsule

Imagine finding long-buried information from your ancestors. That's what a time capsule is—a collection of everyday items stowed or buried away, sometimes for years! It's like finding pieces of history.

Historians did that when they found the oldest known time capsule in the United States, which was created by Samuel Adams and Paul Revere in 1795. Working beneath the Massachusetts State House in 2014, engineers and art conservators found and excavated a brass box inside the building's cornerstone. But the original time capsule was covered in lead and cowhide. It had been opened in 1855 with new items added at that time and then reburied.

The brass box was unsealed in 2015. Special care was taken to remove each item using tools like a porcupine quill and a dental pick. Besides 5 newspapers, over 20 coins were found, one dating back to 1652 and called a pine tree shilling. One noteworthy item was a silver engraved plaque assumed to be made by Paul Revere. Interestingly, Revere's father had emigrated from France to the United States when he was 13 years old. His last name was originally Revoire, but he changed it after establishing his silversmith business in Massachusetts.

More items were added to the Revere-Adams time capsule, including a set of 2015 presidential coins, before it was ceremoniously reburied in a stainless-steel box.

Silver engraving believed to have been created by Paul Revere, found in a 1795 time capsule. *MFA Images, Museum of Fine Arts, Boston*

YOU'LL NEED

* A shoebox or other plastic, metal, or glass container or box

* Personal items from you or your family

* Items representing life in your city, state, or country

1. Decide which container to use for your time capsule. If you plan to bury it or put it somewhere where it will be exposed to water or weather, it should be airtight and watertight.

2. Decide if your time capsule will be personal, show life in general, or be some combination of the two.

3. Think about how long you want your time capsule to go unopened and what to include.

4. Ask your parents about items you plan to put away.

5. Including something with the date in your time capsule will let others know when it was created. Do you want to include items that reflect technology, like an old cell phone or iPod? What about adding copies of school papers or school items? Perhaps you'll write a letter about your life or your family. Fill your time capsule with the items you've selected.

6. Bury or put away your time capsule. Write yourself a note or tell others where you put it and when you plan to open it.

7. And now the hard part—don't open your time capsule until the date you set!

from their ships anyone not eligible under US laws. Railroads sold tickets only to those able to enter the United States legally. The United States put inspectors at Canadian seaports, and beginning in 1895, Canadian officials distributed "Certificates of Admission." These certificates indicated that arrivals had been quarantined, inspected, and granted admittance.

People continued arriving from across the globe, including Slavs, Russian Jews, Greeks, Syrians, and West Indians. French Canadians headed to the United States as well. As before, most were young men. Some had left their families and home countries as a last resort. Estimates indicate that by the late 1800s, 95 percent of Greek immigrants and almost 80 percent of Italian immigrants were men. Many came in the spring, with plans to return to their home country before winter. These workers often performed seasonal jobs, in agriculture or the building trades, and regularly traveled between their home countries and the United States as work required.

As immigration increased, a growing number of politicians, government officials, and journalists took a stand. In 1897 opponents of immigration pushed Congress to require a literacy test for immigrants. But President Grover Cleveland vetoed it. People in favor of positive immigration reform often clashed with those who favored tightening admission criteria, people known as **restrictionists**.

WHITE STAR LINE
TRIPLE SCREW STEAMER
882½ FT. LONG   "OLYMPIC"   46,359 TONS

White Star Line postcards like this helped advertise for business, ca. 1910–1915. *Courtesy of the Library of Congress*

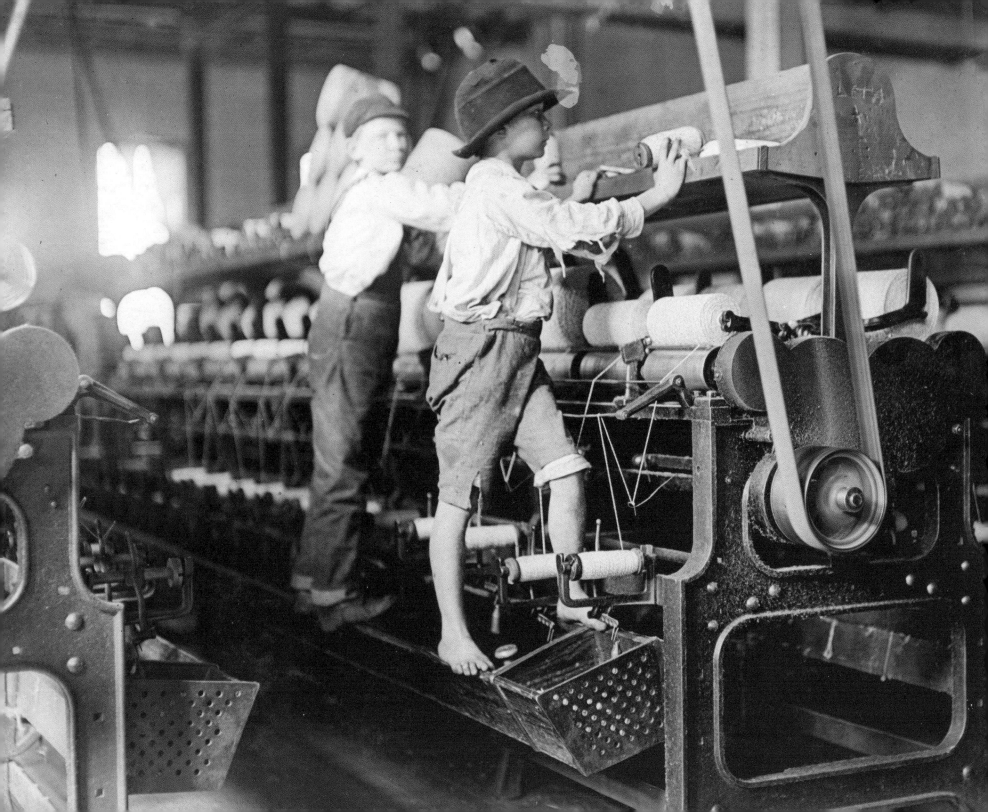

Immigration Changes the United States Forever

—

"Nearly any hour on the East Side of New York City you can see them—pallid boy or spindling girl—their faces dulled, their backs bent under a heavy load of garments piled on head and shoulders, the muscles of the whole frame in a long strain. The boy always has bowlegs and walks with feet apart and wobbling.... Once at home, the little worker sits close to the inadequate window, struggling with the snarls of the thread or shoving the needle through unyielding cloth.... And for this lifting of burdens, this giving of youth and strength, this sacrifice of all that childhood should make radiant, a child may add to the family purse from 50 cents to $1.50 a week."

—Edwin Markham, American poet and journalist, January 1907

With the end of the 1800s, immigration numbers climbed. Reconstruction after the 1897 fire at Ellis Island was completed in 1900, just in time. In addition, Congress enacted several laws to exclude certain people from entering the United States,

Boys at the Bibbs Mill, No. 1, in Macon, Georgia, would climb onto the spinning frame to mend broken threads and replace empty bobbins. *Photo by Lewis Hine. Courtesy of the National Child Labor Committee Collection, Library of Congress, Prints and Photographs Division.*

including individuals with mental or physical defects that might prevent them from earning a living.

Record Numbers Reach American Shores

By 1900, the foreign-born population of New York city reached 37 percent. Other large cities also saw unprecedented numbers. Warsaw—Poland's capital—was the only city in the world with more Poles than Chicago.

The month of April 1907 saw a huge increase in immigrants, with 250,000 arriving on 197 ships. On April 17, 11,747 immigrants arrived—Ellis Island's largest single-day total. Immigrant processing normally took several hours, but those who arrived that day waited several more hours to be examined. As before, immigrants from southern and eastern European countries, like Italy, comprised the majority of arrivals. Almost 81 percent of the 1,285,349 Europeans who arrived in 1907 came from those countries.

Many immigrants were children traveling alone. The Immigration Act of 1907 required that children under the age of 16 be held in detention until a special inquiry hearing determined their fate. Immigration officials attempted to connect children with family members, but often religious or immigrant aid societies took responsibility for them. Other minors began life in the United States thanks to organizations, such as the Hebrew Immigrant Aid Society, which sponsored their travel. Thousands continued their travels on "orphan trains" that took them to prearranged homes in other parts of the country, where they were adopted.

An anti-Italian cartoon published in *Judge* magazine, 1903. *Courtesy of Wikimedia Commons*

Immigrant Children Assume New Roles

Typically, immigrants settled in areas with people of their same ethnicity. Areas such as Chinatown, Little Italy, Greektown, and Little Germany sprang up across the country. People in these communities shared a common language, ethnic food, and cultural and religious beliefs. Sometimes entire villages from one country lived in the same neighborhood. Foreign-language newspapers informed people of issues affecting them in particular. This sense of community helped people survive.

In the early 1900s, immigrant children played an increasingly important role in a country where laws, language, and just about everything differed.

Branch Out and Create a Family Tree

Families come in all shapes and sizes. Whatever your family looks like, you can trace your ancestry back to past generations.

Think about your family—parents, sisters, brothers, grandparents. Deceased family members are also part of your family. A family tree can be large or small, and some go back hundreds of years.

YOU'LL NEED

* Unlined paper
* Pencil or pen
* Colored markers, pencils, or crayons
* Craft supplies (optional)

1. Draw or photocopy the family tree to the right, or use the one in the book. You probably will have to modify the tree for your particular family—every family is different. Color and decorate your family tree however you want.

2. Fill in as much information as you can. You might not be able to fill all the boxes, or you might need more boxes, depending on the size of your family.

3. If you know a family member's birthdate, fill that in.

4. If one of your family members has died, fill in the date if you know it.

5. Can you expand the tree to include your great-grandparents?

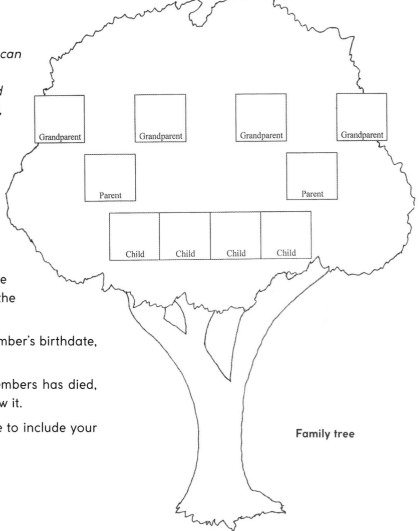

Grandparent Grandparent Grandparent Grandparent

Parent Parent

Child Child Child Child

Family tree

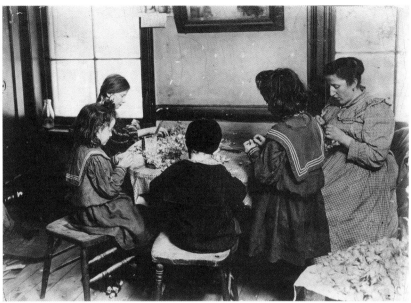

Children tended to learn English more quickly and often took over parental roles. They haggled over prices at markets for bread, cabbage, and fish and dealt with landlords about rent and other issues. Many of them also worked, sometimes 10- or 12-hour days, to help their families survive.

Most parents recognized the importance of education. That was why many immigrants came to the United States—to give their children a better life. Parents usually tried to keep their children in school, at least until they legally obtained working papers at age 14. Most children that age and older worked full-time. But when times were tough or if a family issue arose, such as a parent being unable to work, even very young children missed school temporarily to work. Although factories were not supposed to hire younger children, laws were broken or employers looked the other way.

"Newsies" were children who collected newspapers in the middle of the night and sold them on street corners before school. Children shined shoes, made deliveries, or hauled coal or wood. At home they made artificial flowers, rolled cigars, or sewed buttons on pants. Small home-based factories, including nonfamily members, were no better than larger sweatshops, which were factories or businesses that employed many immigrants. Wages were low, hours were long, and usually working conditions were poor, especially for child workers. Hine compared these situations to child slavery.

Immigrant children in rural areas were sometimes hired out as farmhands on neighboring farms. One 1910 New Jersey labor review reported that the average age for child cranberry pickers was 8 to 10 years old. Another study noted that one-quarter of agricultural workers were younger than 10. But many immigrants believed American life outweighed the violence, oppression, and persecution they faced in their native countries.

Despite hardships, kids still found time to play. In cities, they played in the streets, on fire escapes, or on front porch steps—stoops, as they were called. Typical play included football, baseball, and jump rope. Without money for toys, kids used old hats or discarded items for bases and made wagons out of fruit crates and old wheels.

The Immigration Station in the West

Immigration on the Pacific Coast also faced challenges. At Angel Island, which opened near San Francisco on January 21, 1910, policies and processing were less about welcoming newcomers and more about restriction and rejection. Angel Island presented challenges for Chinese immigrants in particular, who had already been subject to exclusion. This "Ellis Island of the West," as it has been called, became more an island of tears than of joy.

One major difference between the two immigration stations was the segregated facilities at Angel Island, based on ethnicity rather than class. During processing at Angel Island, European men and women, Asian women and children, and Asian men were kept apart. This racist segregation extended to recreation areas, dining facilities, hospital wards, and dormitories—sleeping areas that usually provided bunks for large numbers of people. First-class passengers here received little more than a visual check in their rooms.

Angel Island differed from Ellis Island in other ways too. The food served to Asian people at Angel Island was inferior, and less money was given to the private companies supplying meals for Asians than those providing meals for Europeans or employees. Hospital entrances and stairways were separated, as were patient wards. Sanitary conditions were poor, and the space lacked good toilet facilities, access to hot water, and proper ventilation. Detained Chinese immigrants and other Asian immigrants were not allowed visitors, but other **detainees** could have carefully regulated visits from friends and attorneys on Saturdays and from family members on Sundays.

But the most significant differences involved detention and processing. Chinese and Asian men, women, and children were more often detained

Dormitory at Angel Island. *Courtesy of the Jon B. Lovelace Collection of California Photographs in Carol M. Highsmith's America Project, Library of Congress, Prints and Photographs Division*

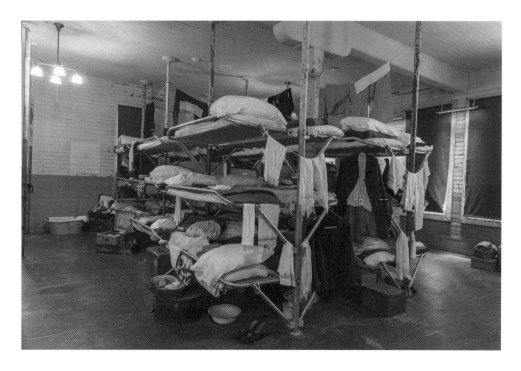

Chinese poetic verse carved into the wall of the detention barracks at Angel Island, San Francisco, California. *Courtesy of the Jon B. Lovelace Collection of California Photographs in Carol M. Highsmith's America Project, Library of Congress, Prints and Photographs Division*

and spent longer periods at Angel Island. While 20 percent of Ellis Island arrivals were detained—some for only one night—60 percent of Angel Island immigrants faced at least three days' detention. On average, about 38 percent of non-Asians required further inspection, whereas about 76 percent of all Chinese immigrants did.

Detention meant confined, prison-like facilities for Chinese people, except for meals or two exercise periods a day. Chinese women were allowed daily walks, but only under guard. With cramped and dirty dormitories, it is understandable why many Chinese detainees expressed frustration and anger when interviewed years later. Numerous Chinese poems written and carved into barracks' walls at Angel Island have been discovered, many expressing anguish and sadness about their treatment. Historical records note that Black immigrants from Africa and elsewhere also faced discrimination while coming to America.

Medical examinations also differed for Chinese and Asian immigrants. Scientists then believed Asians carried infections that targeted White Americans. Asians were required to fully undress and give stool and urine samples to be tested for bacteria, practices they found extremely embarrassing. Their eyes were carefully examined. But even though Europeans tended to be more susceptible to infections, more Asians and Middle Eastern immigrants were diagnosed with infections and targeted for deportation. Since a laborer's hands would typically be discolored or have calluses, even the hands of Asian men claiming to be merchants were inspected.

When the 1906 San Francisco earthquake destroyed most of the city's birth certificates, it was easier for people to claim exemption from immigration restrictions as Chinese American citizens. So officials added rules to make it harder to get around immigration laws, especially for paper sons and daughters. Now, even merchants and others exempt from exclusion laws needed a government certificate to prove their eligibility for entry.

Immigration officials then compared the information on the certificates with the information in government files. People without certification had to have a witness back up their claim. Many Chinese immigrants were suspected of arranging with "witnesses" for illegal entry. One Secret Service agent reported as far back as 1899 that "San Francisco is full of old men, that will, for $5, identify ANY Chinaman as his son." In fact, an underground business of selling certificates existed in China and the United States.

Knowing this, officials devised ways to trap people. Witnesses and immigrants were interviewed separately and asked specific questions. Families, in particular, were carefully scrutinized, with husbands and wives questioned separately. Besides routine immigration questions, Angel Island arrivals answered questions about everything from the number of stairs leading to their houses to whether the name above the door of the village hall was painted or carved. Relatives traveling together were asked the same questions. The slightest differences in answers gave grounds for deportation. For Chinese immigrants, questioning

How Do Your Family Members Match Up?

West Coast immigration officials asked Chinese family members the same questions. Many were simply about their home, neighborhood, or village and had nothing to do with how they might contribute positively to American life.

If you had to answer questions and match answers with family members, how well would you do?

YOU'LL NEED

* Paper, lined or unlined
* Pencils or pens
* One or more family members

1. Both you and your family members should write down your answers to the following questions without sharing them. While these are not real questions asked of Chinese immigrants, you'll understand how easy or hard it was for family members to answer the same questions. Imagine that you might be denied entry if your answers don't match.

2. When you're done, compare your responses. How well did you match up? Can you think of other questions?

1. How many stairs lead into your house?
2. How many windows are on the ground floor of your home?
3. How many rugs are in your bathroom?
4. What color are your living room curtains?
5. What do the dinner plates you eat on look like?
6. How many televisions do you have in your home?
7. How many drawers are in your kitchen?
8. How many shelves are in your refrigerator?
9. How many rooms are in your house, excluding the basement and attic?
10. How many doors lead to the outside from your house?

could take several days and might mean up to 50 pages of written testimony. Records indicate that in one extreme case, a Chinese applicant was asked 900 questions.

While these questions might have satisfied inspectors with their thoroughness, that was not always true. Answers to expected questions were sold in coaching books or passed on to new arrivals in food packages. Legitimate applicants whose answers differed even slightly from those of their family members might be denied entry, but those who memorized answers well enough might pass. Even corrupt inspectors participated in the scheme.

Many desperate immigrants felt their only choice was to take this "crooked path." Even though they gained entry to a new life, many were constantly fearful of discovery and deportation.

Immigrants Answer the Call

Prior to World War I, immigrants to the United States from countries like Russia, Bulgaria, Serbia, and Turkey increased. Many arrivals fled political upheaval or religious persecution or feared mandatory military service. But what also followed was an increase in the number of people returning home, many of whom worried that if the United States waged war, restrictions might prevent them from going back.

Several federal immigration laws at the time affected immigrants worldwide. The IRL and other restrictionists again pushed for a literacy bill but were unsuccessful. Finally, during Woodrow Wilson's presidency in 1917, restrictionists in Congress overrode the president's veto and literacy was added to the immigration requirements. Because literacy rates in southeastern European countries were considerably lower than those in northwestern European countries, this bill omitted certain immigrants without appearing openly racist.

The Immigration Act of 1917 required anyone 16 years or older to read 30 to 40 words in a language of their choice, usually their native language. In addition, they had to read a passage from the Bible or another religious prayer book. Arnold Weiss, a 13-year-old Russian immigrant in the 1930s, recalled ducking down and whispering the words from a Jewish prayer book, which he had memorized, to his mother who pretended to read. She passed the literacy test.

Alcoholics and people with certain mental disorders were banned from entering the United States, along with immigrants older than 16 years old who were considered physically handicapped or mentally defective. Homosexuals who admitted their sexuality were considered mentally defective. The law also barred immigrants from several Asian countries, as well as Mexican and Mediterranean immigrants. This law, which had 38 sections, was one of the most restrictive immigration laws ever enacted in the United States. It remained in effect for 35 years until its repeal in 1952. Some issues, such as the exclusion of homosexuals, remained in effect for even longer.

THE SOLUTION TO INTELLIGENCE TESTING

By doing a quick visible check of immigrants, doctors found most physical defects, but finding mental issues took more investigation. Some signs for possible mental problems, such as excitability for no obvious reason or the inability to stay focused for too long, were obvious, but others were not. In addition, immigration laws allowed no leeway for certain individuals, including those called idiots and the feeble-minded.

But doctors recognized that external factors such as fatigue, seasickness, the stress of travel, and even processing affected results. Eventually, immigrants requiring further examination were first fed, given a bath, and allowed to sleep prior to testing. Doctors also addressed testing room temperatures, ventilation, and noise levels.

The Binet test, created by French psychologist Alfred Binet, rated a person's comprehension and reasoning. This test improved on previous intelligence tests based on craniometry, or the physical dimension of a person's skull. Eventually, Ellis Island doctors recognized that intelligence tests were sometimes slanted against certain immigrants. For example, one test involved a picture showing three sad children putting flowers on their pet rabbit's grave. First, many immigrants had little connection to pictures. Second, many immigrants never kept rabbits as pets. Last, putting flowers on a grave was something many immigrants had never experienced. It is understandable that some "failed" this test.

Ellis Island doctors developed nonverbal tests. One involved putting wooden shapes into boards with matching cutout pieces. The Feature Profile Test, developed by Howard Knox and used from 1912 to 1916, was a puzzle with wooden pieces resembling facial features everyone recognized. The Knox Imitation Cube Test involved cubes placed 4 inches (10.1 cm) apart and touched in a specific pattern that immigrants had to repeat. Although people could argue against the unfairness of excluding certain immigrants, Ellis Island doctors created a fairer test that still followed the law.

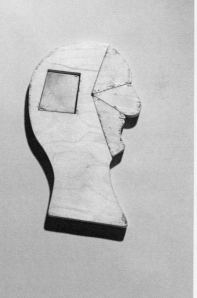

Feature Profile Test given to Ellis Island immigrants as part of their intelligence testing, with completed puzzle. © *Stephen Lewis*

FRUITS
AND
VEGETABLES
I AM AN AMERICAN
WANTO CO.
WANTO CO.
VEGETABLES
PHILIP
MORRIS

World Crises and the US Response

8

"I wanted to show something, to contribute to America. My parents could not become citizens but they told me 'You fight for your country.'"

—Minoru Hinahara, Nisei Japanese American, US 27th Army Division, World War II

Once the United States entered World War I, immigration numbers in the East dropped. Safety was a factor, since Germany threatened attacks on steamships that it suspected of carrying supplies to Europe. US immigration, averaging about one million arrivals annually, dropped to just over 110,000 arrivals in 1918. The United States suspended travel back to countries engaged in war, so detainees faced more uncertainty.

Sign in a storefront window in Oakland, California, the day of the bombing at Pearl Harbor.
Courtesy of the Library of Congress

Many immigrants showed their patriotism and volunteered for the military. About 18 percent of US soldiers were immigrants. The 77th Infantry Division, called the "Melting Pot Division" because many members came from New York City, was one of several units that included immigrants. Its helmet had an image of the Statue of Liberty.

Many immigrants who joined the military did not speak English or had no knowledge of US laws or government affairs. The military offered them English and history classes, along with ones in basic skills like cooking, sewing, and childcare. The government's belief was that this education would prepare these people for life both on and off the battlefield. On May 9, 1918, Congress enacted a law that allowed immigrants in the armed services to become naturalized citizens by having two witnesses and proof of military enlistment. The law also removed the five-year residency requirement, did not require immigrants to speak English, and did away with the need to take history and civics exams. Volunteer attorneys and servicemen served as examiners to speed up the process on some military bases and judges were often sent to perform outside, open-air naturalization ceremonies. Enlisted immigrants could be processed within one day, and these changes allowed over 300,000 immigrants to become citizens. For others, they made the ultimate sacrifice—giving their lives for a country where they were not yet citizens.

War Fears Turn Inward

During the war, Ellis Island and Angel Island served as detention centers for prisoners of war. Shortly after entering the war, President Wilson used the Alien Enemies Act to round up, imprison, and deport unnaturalized adult men considered alien enemies. Wilson expanded this on April 6, 1917, by declaring that any male Germans who were 14 years old or older and not naturalized could be targeted as alien enemies. Immediately, Germans who fit the criteria were rounded up and transported to Ellis Island.

In cities like Hoboken, New Jersey, with a large German population, ethnic neighborhoods felt the effects of these rules. German people working on German steamships docked at American ports also went to Ellis Island. About 1,500 Germans spent time there before being transferred

77th Infantry Division helmet showing the Statue of Liberty. *The National WWI Museum and Memorial*

Instructors teaching English to World War I veterans, with copies of *A Foreigner's Guide to English* on the table. *Courtesy of the George Grantham Bain Collection, Library of Congress*

to detention camps in North Carolina. Another three dozen Germans, charged with spying for the enemy, remained at Ellis Island before transfer.

Alien enemies residing in the United States, German seamen working on American or German shipping vessels, passengers arriving from enemy countries, radicals and anarchists viewed as threats to national security, and Germans transferred from other locations like the Philippines, all resided at Angel Island. Most of them were eventually transferred to North Carolina.

With an increase in patriotism during World War I, hostility toward Germans and those of German ancestry rose to new levels, speared on by stories about German actions during the war. Because some Irish immigrants hoped a German victory would result in Ireland's independence if Britain lost, many Americans held strong feelings against the Irish.

Russians also were singled out, especially after the reigning Russian Romanov family was murdered. Because labor strikes were on the rise, the press and others blamed immigrants for this movement. People feared Communism would make its way into American life. This "Red Scare" raised old fears of the number of antigovernment individuals increasing and threatening the country. A series of bombings by anarchists fueled the fire.

During the war, Ellis Island played a role when 249 men and women were rounded up from ports across the East Coast and detained there. These mostly Russian and German detainees were awakened before dawn on a snowy morning, December 21, 1919, and transferred to a waiting troopship

A group of Germans from Hoboken, New Jersey, awaiting deportation, 1917. *Courtesy of the George Grantham Bain Collection, Library of Congress*

for deportation. Many had been rounded up the night of November 7 in what became known as the Palmer Raids. Over several months, thousands of suspected anarchists were detained. Most were released because they were not Communists or because they were denied certain legal rights, such as having an attorney with them while being questioned. Eventually, a report exposed the wrongs of the Department of Justice, including its physical abuse of these detainees.

Added to this was a reemergence of the Ku Klux Klan, a group started in 1865 by Confederate veterans opposed to programs pushing equality for African Americans. The original Klan, a secret underground organization that spread to every southern state, pushed for White supremacy. While the group's influence waned at the end of the 19th century, it saw a regrowth in the early 1920s. The new Klan opposed Jews, Catholics, labor unions, and foreigners, along with African Americans. Made up of law enforcement officials, ministers, and successful community members, it promoted violence. Wearing hooded white robes and staging parades and marches, the Klan used a burning cross as its symbol and instituted a reign of terror in every state, but particularly in the South. Although its numbers have decreased since it boasted 4 million members in the 1920s, the Klan today bills itself as the leading voice for White supremacy.

The Federal Government Plays Its Hand

At the same time, the US federal government took a stand that would affect the country for decades. Although stories prevailed about immigrants flooding US shores, data proved otherwise. About 430,000 immigrants arrived from 1919 to 1920, but 290,000 returned home. Still, with anti-immigrant sentiment high, the government enacted its first quota system, based on the census of 1910.

A bill was proposed by Congressman Albert Johnson of Washington, who feared the purity of the United States would be tainted by immigrant races, especially if they intermarried with White people. Johnson was anti-Semitic, meaning anti-Jewish. The Immigration Act of 1921, also called the Emergency Quota Act, not only limited the number of immigrants admitted annually, but also assigned the percentage or quota of immigrants allowed in—initially 3 percent—based on people from certain nationalities already here. Countries in the Western Hemisphere—most notably Canada and Mexico—had no quotas. The total number allowed in came to just over 350,000 new arrivals.

One of the law's most restrictive rules allowed no more than 20 percent of one country's annual quota admitted in any one-month period. Even if bad weather delayed their departure, people arriving once the maximum had been reached were deported or denied entry. This bill included a provision basing quota percentages on the most current census data every 10 years. Thousands of people attempted to beat the date the law would officially be enacted. Before the June 3, 1921, midnight deadline, 11 ships jockeyed into position to cross an imaginary line in New York Harbor patrolled by immigration officials.

After the deadline, entire ships were refused if a country's quota had been met. Depending on people already admitted, family members might be denied entry if their country of origin had reached its quota, while others could enter. Fathers, wives, mothers, husbands, sons, daughters, and extended family members sometimes faced the heartbreak of separation, simply because of where they were born.

Since the new law was meant to be a temporary answer, Congress extended the expiration date for the Immigration Act of 1921 to June 30, 1924. Congress then enacted the Immigration Act of 1924, reinstituting many of the 1921 restrictions—only tougher. Instead of using 1910 census data for determining quotas, figures were now based on the 1890 census, which highly favored immigrants from northwestern Europe.

This new act limited the number of individuals from each country to 2 percent of those in the United States according to that census. The annual quota for all nations was limited to 153,714. Nations in the Western Hemisphere were exempt, and Asians were already excluded by earlier laws.

Another aspect of the law had an impact on Ellis Island. It required American consulates worldwide to examine **visa** applicants, including for physical and mental health. Because these immigrants were already examined before they arrived in the United States, the number of immigrants needing extensive examinations at Ellis Island dropped to about 1 percent. Another change—examining paperwork and providing medical examinations on the ships—also reduced the amount of processing at Ellis Island.

Some people argued that previously exempted Western Hemisphere countries—mainly Canada and Mexico—should be included in the new law and quota limits applied. But most people felt that people crossing from Canada into the United States illegally would not affect the racial balance of the United States. And because Mexican workers were in high demand in railroad and agricultural industries, their numbers should not be limited. With the continued exclusion of Asians, the need for agricultural workers increased the number of **undocumented immigrants** crossing into the United States, particularly along the Mexico-US border.

The United States Defends Its Southwestern Border

Congress took steps to guard almost 2,000 miles (3,219 km) of its southwestern border by creating the Border Patrol in 1924. Officially created by federal law, mounted US Immigration Service guards have patrolled the border since 1904. The original focus of these Mounted Guards, as they were called, was to capture undocumented Chinese immigrants. But with the amount of territory to patrol, which in 1925 expanded to the California coastline, there were rarely enough border agents. Patrol agents furnished their own horses and saddles. The federal government supplied oats and hay for the horses, along with a revolver and badge to their riders. In future years the role of the Border Patrol expanded.

While immigration numbers dropped dramatically during World War I, quota requirements played a greater role in changing immigration numbers. The new law achieved restrictionists' goals of reducing the number of immigrants from countries in southern and eastern Europe. By the mid-1920s, immigrants arriving from countries in the favored Western Hemisphere increased dramatically.

Chinese immigrants continued to take advantage of the paper son and daughter exemption—legally or illegally. Other arrivals found a simpler way to enter the United States by obtaining a visitor's visa and not returning home when it expired. This practice is still commonly used today.

The United States Reverses Course Again

One unforeseen factor that affected immigration was the Great Depression. Although the United States had faced depressions before, the stock

How Did Ethnicity Change?

As the numbers of immigrants increased from 1880 to 1920, the ethnicity of those immigrants changed too. This led to more concerns about immigrant populations and how to restrict those people considered undesirable. Of special concern were certain populations from Europe. Eventually, those opposed to immigration pushed for tighter controls, leading to quotas, which you'll read about in this chapter.

YOU'LL NEED

* Census chart (p. 87)
* Pencil or pen
* Ruler
* Calculator (optional)
* Colored marker, pencil, or crayon

1. Draw or photocopy the census chart on page 87, or use the one in the book.

2. Use the calculator or your brain to add up the numbers for each geographical area (northwestern Europe, central Europe, etc.). Some numbers are done for you. Put the total in the appropriate box. Do this for all decades. (Completed tables are on page 123.)

3. Because of rounding, the numbers may not add up to 100 percent for each decade.

4. Color the box with the largest percentage of immigrants for each decade—one box in each column.

5. How did ethnicity change from decade to decade?

6. How do numbers for northwestern and southeastern Europe compare?

7. How do you think these changes affected government regulations after 1920, including the quota system?

IMMIGRATION TO THE UNITED STATES BY DECADE				
Country	1880-1889	1890-1899	1900-1909	1910-1919
United Kingdom	15.5	8.9	5.7	5.8
Ireland	12.8	11.0	4.2	2.6
Scandinavia	12.7	10.5	5.9	3.8
France	0.9	1.0	0.4	1.0
German Empire	27.5	15.7	4.0	2.7
Other	2.9	2.3	1.4	1.6
Northwestern Europe TOTALS				
Poland	0.8	2.9	0.0	18.2
Austria-Hungary	6.0	14.5	24.4	0.4
Other	0.0	0.0	0.4	0.0
Central Europe TOTALS				
Russia	3.5	12.7	18.3	17.4
Romania	0.1	0.2	0.7	0.2
Turkey in Europe	0.0	0.1	0.8	1.1
Greece	0.0	0.3	1.8	3.1
Italy	5.1	16.3	23.5	19.4
Spain	0.1	0.2	0.3	0.8
Portugal	0.3	0.7	0.8	1.3
Southeastern Europe TOTALS				
Asia	1.3	1.5	2.9	3.1
Central and South America	9.9	1.1	3.4	16.9
Other countries	0.2	0.5	0.6	0.5

market crash on October 24, 1929, marked the worst of them. Still, about 70,000 more people arrived than left over the next 10 years.

During the Depression, Mexican farmworkers were especially hard hit. Some states and local communities held "**repatriation drives**" to round up Mexicans, pack them onto buses, trucks, or trains, and deport them. In California, even hospitalized people suspected of being Mexicans were included. People suffering from leprosy, mental illness, tuberculosis, and other medical or age-related problems were transported to the Mexican border and discharged.

No federal law authorized these raids, but Mexican American citizens as well as documented and undocumented immigrants, including women and children, were rounded up in states across the country. Former California state senator Joseph Dunn estimated that about 1.8 million Mexicans were **repatriated**—60 percent of whom he believes were American citizens. His family was among those deported. Other reports indicate numbers as low as 400,000 and as high as 2 million. And although Mexicans had the option of leaving voluntarily—and many did—even the US federal government later reported that these efforts included forceful tactics.

President Herbert Hoover didn't take a stand, but his campaign slogan, "American Jobs for Real Americans," underscored his beliefs. At the time, many large US corporations, including one railroad that had previously welcomed Mexican workers, laid off thousands of Mexicans. Repatriation lasted until about 1939.

In 2005, Dunn helped promote and pass an act apologizing for repatriation. He explained the challenges these people faced when he said, "That is the tragedy. . . . Most of the deportees in [the]

1930s that were shipped to Mexico did not speak the language. And they were not only thrown out of their country of birth, the United States, they were foreigners in the new land that they were shipped to, that being Mexico."

In 1933, responsibility for immigration and naturalization oversight was combined. The Bureau of Naturalization and the Bureau of Immigration became the Immigration and Naturalization Service.

At the same time Mexicans faced deportation, Filipinos were targeted. It began with an event that many Filipinos likely celebrated. The Tydings-McDuffie Act of March 1934 granted the Philippines status as a commonwealth. The country would achieve independence after 10 years, which officially occurred on July 4, 1946.

With the signed law, the United States now considered the Philippines a separate nation and applied immigration quotas as with other countries. Unfortunately, the Philippines quota was 50 immigrants. Even more detrimental, the law separated families by excluding wives and children of those granted entry.

In addition, the law changed the status of Filipinos, even those already in the United States, from nationals to aliens. Like with Mexicans, the government pushed repatriation. However, because the Filipinos traveled to their homeland by steamship, they were detained at Angel Island until there was a large enough group for deportation. There were numerous complaints of Filipinos being mistreated and abused at Angel Island. Conditions were intolerable, and sick people needing

MEXICAN LABORERS FILL THE GAP

The Bracero Program was the largest foreign worker program in American history, involving 4.5 to 5 million Mexican workers in 24 states. The program granted temporary labor contracts to fill the gap at factories and on farms because of labor shortages during World War II.

The first workers arrived on September 27, 1942. Workers were promised a 30-cents-an-hour wage, adequate food, sanitary shelter, and protection from discrimination at Whites-only establishments. In reality, they suffered racial discrimination and abuse. Barns were sometimes converted into housing that lacked sanitary facilities and running water.

Workers in the Pacific Northwest staged work stoppages and strikes, knowing that the distance to the Mexican border made deportation more difficult. But the program was still accused of abuse by people like Cesar Chavez, who successfully fought for farmworkers' rights.

What nobody likely expected was that the program actually fueled illegal immigration. Some in the agricultural industry found it easier and quicker to hire undocumented workers. By the end of the program, more undocumented workers had entered the United States than those who legally participated.

Interestingly, the US Department of Labor established a program to fill the void when the Bracero Program ended. It failed miserably. A-TEAM, or Athletes in Temporary Employment as Agricultural Manpower, expected to replace at least 20,000 Mexican workers by recruiting male high school athletes to perform agricultural work during the summer, even though farmers had previously complained that Americans didn't want these jobs. Fewer than 3,500 students were enlisted, many of whom soon quit because of the difficult work, low wages, poor living conditions, and oppressive heat.

hospitalization had to pay for it themselves. Over three years, almost 2,200 Filipinos were deported.

War Raises the Stakes for Many Immigrants

Immigration in the East increased as people from Nazi Germany and particularly Jews sought status as refugees. Unfortunately, the Immigration Act of 1924 had no provisions allowing quotas to be waived or changed even for extreme need. Throughout the 1930s, and after 1938 when Adolf Hitler intensified anti-Semitic propaganda, the need for leeway on quotas became more apparent. President Franklin D. Roosevelt called other countries to an international conference in July 1938 to discuss immigration. But most of the 32 countries attending refused to increase numbers of immigrants from countries under Hitler's influence. The United States was among them, even though the number of people waiting for quota visas by 1939 had risen to over 300,000, with at least a two-year wait.

Eventually, Roosevelt's labor secretary, Frances Perkins, convinced him to give 12,000 Germans already in the United States temporary visitor visas indefinitely. But, when a bill was introduced to allow 20,000 German children under age 14 entry above quota limitations, the proposal was never voted on. The argument was that allowing that many children to enter would adversely affect jobs available to American *children*. Although the United States accepted more refugees from Nazi-controlled countries, the vast majority of people

Mexican migrant workers brought to the United States to harvest and process sugar beets, 1943. *Courtesy of the Farm Security Administration, Library of Congress*

turned away likely ended up in concentration camps.

On the other side of the country, fire broke out on Angel Island on August 12, 1940. Blamed on faulty writing, the inferno destroyed much of the administration building. The federal government then decided to close the facility.

About this time, with the United States on the threshold of another war, farmers became increasingly worried about the need for foreign farmworkers. When the United States entered the war in 1941, Mexico soon joined the fight and considered supplying cheap labor as one way to help the war effort. But because its citizens had been abused and discriminated against before, Mexico outlined specific requirements. The agreement, officially enacted on August 4, 1942, became known as the Bracero Program, referring to the Spanish word for a manual or farm laborer. The program, renewed or extended eight times until 1964, kept the United States supplied with food and workers. Approximately 4.6 million people came from Mexico during the program's 22-year history, with many eventually attaining legal status and making the United States their home.

The United States Takes Up Arms

After the United States entered World War II on December 8, 1941, some 7,000 Filipino people served in the military, in spite of repatriation. Two Filipino regiments were formed in 1942, and the Philippines and the United States became allies fighting side by side.

The day after the Pearl Harbor bombing, the United States issued a proclamation naming any non-naturalized Germans, Italians, or Japanese as alien enemies. Within a day, almost 2,500 individuals were arrested. Another 2,200 faced that same action the next day. Though many were released, others went to Ellis Island for detention.

About 13,000 individuals with Chinese ancestry, about 60 percent of them native-born Chinese Americans, joined the war effort. Their prospects improved because China supported the Allies during the war. The repeal of the Chinese Exclusion Act in 1943 finally gave these people a path to citizenship. Approximately 10,000 Chinese women married to American citizens were permitted to enter the United States without counting against quota admissions.

But the people most profoundly affected by anti-immigration attitudes, particularly in the West, were the Japanese. Although immigration from Japan had all but ended, almost 250,000 Japanese people lived in Hawaii and the United States. By 1940, the number of children who were US citizens born to Japanese immigrants—called Nisei—totaled almost 63 percent of children of Japanese heritage.

With anti-Japanese feelings rising amid rumors of them helping their homeland and interrupting US war efforts, Roosevelt signed an executive order on February 19, 1942, requiring those of Japanese heritage—citizens or not—to be rounded up and transferred to 10 internment camps in some of the remotest areas of the United States. Historians have called these places little more than concentration camps. This internment program affected more than 120,000 Japanese Americans. About 80,000 of these people were citizens, and some remained interned for up to four years until the last camp closed in March 1946.

Honouliuli internment camp, Hawaii, 1945. *Courtesy of the US National Park Service*

Still, some 3,600 Nisei interned at camps volunteered for US military service, along with more than 22,000 living in Hawaii. One Nisei military group, the 442nd Regimental Combat Team, became one of the most decorated units in World War II history.

In 1988 the US government tried to rectify these injustices when President Ronald Reagan signed a bill apologizing for the government's role. Financial compensation of $20,000 was awarded to each individual still alive who had lived in these camps.

One little-known event in US immigration history is the creation of a **refugee camp** in Oswego, New York, in 1944. With a push by the Treasury Department, President Roosevelt established the War Refugee Board and soon after approved creation of an Emergency Refugee Shelter at Fort Ontario. In June 1944, 1,000 refugees were chosen out of 3,000 applicants fleeing the Nazis to travel from Naples, Italy, to the United States. In all, 982 refugees arrived and made their home at the converted military camp. People favoring and opposing immigration had mixed feelings about this decision. Although the refugees had agreed to return to Europe after the war, in late 1945, President Harry Truman granted them guest visas allowing them to remain.

Although over one million immigrants arrived at Ellis Island during World War I, the numbers fell from 1942 to 1945. The island was officially called a detention center and housed seamen from enemy ships along with alien enemies.

Create an Immigration Poster

Discussions about immigration sometimes bring up strong feelings. Our history, like that of other countries, has shown that sometimes we've treated immigrants fairly and other times we haven't.

Think about issues you've read about so far and consider US laws. How do you feel about our history concerning immigration?

YOU'LL NEED

* Poster board or large sheet of paper
* Pencil or pen
* Colored markers, pencils, or crayons
* Craft supplies (optional)

1. Pick one event in immigration history.

2. Posters supporting or opposing something often have a catchy slogan that sums up the issue or helps people remember it. Examples in US history are: "Keep Cool with Coolidge" (campaign slogan for Calvin Coolidge) and "Be All You Can Be" (US Army recruiting slogan, 1980–2001). Think of a phrase for your poster.

3. Draw, color, and decorate a poster showing your feelings about an immigration issue.

4. Share your poster with your family and friends and discuss why you feel this way.

9

The United States
Confronts Global Issues Again

—

"Nowadays, sometimes I feel like a frog jumping from one world to the other: school, my friends, being American, being Khmer [Cambodian]. In a way to be assimilated in another culture, you have to give up your own culture. With one foot in each culture, the wider you have to spread your legs, the more you could lose your balance."

—Sathaya Tor, Cambodian refugee, 1981

After World War II, the direction of US immigration changed. With stories of Nazi atrocities in the international news and thousands of people trying to rebuild their lives, more tolerant attitudes prevailed. Although many people had been affected by the physical damages of war, others had been detained in concentration camps or prisons, forced to go on death marches or work as laborers, or had no homes to return

The shrimp boat *El Dorado* overpacked with Cuban refugees and headed to the United States, 1980.
Florida Photographic Collection, State Archives of Florida

to. One of the US federal government's first post-war actions addressed these people.

President Harry Truman signed an executive order instructing American government personnel overseas to continue granting visas, giving preference to people considered **displaced persons** (DPs). This new order allowed only about 41,000 immigrants entry to the United States, mostly from countries with low quota numbers. In a letter written December 22, 1945, Truman requested that these "visas should be distributed fairly among persons of all faiths, creeds, and

Sinaida Grussman holds a name card to help surviving family members locate her at the Kloster Indersdorf DP camp in Germany. *Courtesy of the US Holocaust Memorial Museum*

nationalities. I desire that special attention be devoted to orphaned children to whom it is hoped the majority of visas will be issued."

During the war, the number of immigrants from many European countries had been extremely low. In fact, until the end of November 1945, only about 10 percent of quotas for Europe had been used. And numbers since 1942 had been equal to or less than that. But unused quota visas were not allowed to accumulate for future use. So rather than increasing or relaxing numbers for affected countries, the government allowed countries to "borrow" against future visas. So many people applied for visas from Latvia, a country with 275 slots, that the number of visas requested in the first year used all the quotas allowed until the year 2274.

For the first time in history, the United States passed a law that specifically addressed refugees. The Displaced Persons Act, signed on June 25, 1948, targeted millions of DPs in countries like Germany and Austria. Unfortunately, while Truman pushed for admittance *outside* quota numbers, the law required these visas counted *within* quota totals.

At the time, millions of DPs lived in **refugee camps** in Italy, Germany, and Austria, temporarily set up to help alleviate issues. Many DPs had only recently been freed from concentration camps. Unfortunately, the law prohibited people who entered refugee camps *after* December 22, 1945, from applying for visas. Many Jewish people were ineligible, as were Catholics living in countries under Communist rule who fled after that date.

ANNE FRANK'S FAMILY'S ATTEMPTS TO FIND SAFETY

Anne Frank is known for *The Diary of Anne Frank*, based on her writings during her family's 761 days in hiding from the Nazis in the Netherlands. Stories told after the war about her family being denied entry to the United States were not true, but Frank's story is tragic nonetheless.

Until World War II ended, the German quota for immigrants was 26,000. But from June 1938 to June 1939, the waiting list jumped from about 139,100 people to almost 310,000. Anne Frank's father, Otto Frank, first attempted to emigrate to the United States in 1938. But the family's paperwork was destroyed when the Rotterdam consulate was bombed in May 1940. All applications had to be resubmitted, but it's unknown if Frank followed through or not.

In 1941 family members in German-occupied countries became ineligible for US visas. Shortly after, more government department approvals were needed. Then the Nazis closed all consulates in Germany and occupied lands. This wiped out any chance to go directly to the United States. The Franks attempted to get there by way of Cuba.

On November 25, 1941, German Jews residing outside Germany were stripped of their nationality, leaving them without a country. Then the Franks' immigration application to Cuba was cancelled after the Pearl Harbor bombing, which suspended shipping traffic. In June 1942, Anne, along with her sister and parents, went into hiding.

For years, people believed they were betrayed, perhaps by an employee of Otto Frank. But recent research indicates that the German intelligence police were searching the building in which they were hiding, for unrelated illegal activity. In an attic area, the Germans discovered the Frank family along with four others.

Otto Frank was the only member of his family to survive a concentration camp. Anne and her sister Margot died just months before the war ended.

Anne Frank in a school photograph taken at the Jewish High School Amsterdam, 1941.
Courtesy of Wikimedia Commons

Although the passage of the bill allowed approximately 200,000 refugees in during the first two-year period, the majority of them—some 80 percent—had to be Christians. Truman grudgingly signed the legislation but spent two years pushing Congress for changes. On the day he signed the law, Truman said, "It is with very great reluctance that I have signed S. 2242, the Displaced Persons Act of 1948. . . . It is a close question whether this bill is better or worse than no bill at all. . . . It must be frankly recognized, therefore, that this bill excludes Jewish displaced persons, rather than accepting a fair proportion of them along with other faiths."

Truman finally prevailed in 1950, and the new law removed the date of arrival at refugee camps as a requirement and increased the number of admissions. Again in 1950, the law was amended after much disagreement and discussion, allowing another 200,000 refugees into the United States.

Two Superpowers and the Challenges for Immigrants

Toward the second half of the 20th century, two world superpowers emerged, affecting immigration for decades. Rising tensions between the Soviet Union and the United States reopened old Red Scare concerns. While neither country had an interest in going to war, the Soviet Union flexed its muscles to spread and establish Communist nations. The United States was just as determined to prevent that. Millions of people found themselves caught in this Cold War.

Although the Immigration and Nationality Act of 1952 did not change the policy of allotting quotas, it focused on reuniting families and encouraging skilled immigrants to apply for visas. Professionals, such as doctors and engineers, received special consideration, and family unification gave relatives of permanent US residents or citizens priority, a renewal of the chain migration system. It also allowed Asians to emigrate. Quota numbers were established at one-tenth of 1 percent of the population of different nations based on the 1920 census. No more than 160,000 immigrants from all nationalities around the world could be admitted. In addition, the US president now had

the power to make temporary exemptions to the immigration quota laws and admit extra refugees based on emergency situations, and more refugees were welcomed.

This legislation also addressed the increasing fear of Communism. Aliens or others whose behavior or political ideals were considered detrimental to society could be excluded or deported, including Communist Party members and anarchists. Most of the same individuals barred from entering before, like paupers, were still excluded. The new law laid out 31 different categories that denied someone entry. Truman again vetoed the bill, saying, "The greatest vice of the present quota system . . . is that it discriminates, deliberately and intentionally, against any of the peoples of the world." Both the House and the Senate overrode his veto the following day.

As humanitarian crises continued, in 1953 the United States replaced the expired Displaced Persons Act with the Refugee Relief Act. While some opposed it, the final bill kept the same quota requirements from before. This law allowed entry for just under 215,000 people—mostly refugees and displaced persons—spread over a roughly three-and-a-half year period.

Despite activity as a detention center, particularly during the Korean War, in 1951, Ellis Island's era ended when processing costs outweighed its usefulness. With more and more immigrants traveling by air and visas awarded before departure, the government closed Ellis Island on November 12, 1954. The last and lone detainee was Norwegian sailor Arne Peterssen, who had overstayed his shore leave. He was released to rejoin his crewmates but enjoyed none of the fanfare or fame of Annie Moore.

While many people outside the country leaned more toward tolerance of immigrants, attitudes inside the United States pointed in the opposite direction. "Operation Wetback" was the response to what some people felt was a problematic flood of Mexicans seeking work in the United States. The term is a demeaning reference to the fact that some Mexicans crossed the Rio Grande River to reach the United States. Initiated during the summer of 1954—while the Bracero Program was still in place—Operation Wetback's raids on undocumented immigrants swept through the Southwest and states that attracted laborers. In spite of Truman's earlier objections to Congress's direction on immigration, this program rolled out during his administration.

INS and Border Patrol agents carried out these surprise raids. Mexicans who were caught needed their birth certificate to prove their citizenship but had no time to produce it before being detained. Other papers were not accepted. Individuals were given no legal representation or lawful rights and had no chance to contact family members before being loaded up for deportation. Mexican people were picked up from cattle ranches, citrus farms, hotels, restaurants, factories, and anywhere INS agents thought they'd be working.

This program differed from the earlier one because individuals were now transported hundreds of miles into southern Mexico. Again, many of the deported people were not familiar with

"Whites Only" discrimination sign from Dimmitt, Texas, meant for migrant agricultural workers, 1949. *Russell Lee Photograph Collection, e_rl_14646_0038, The Dolph Briscoe Center for American History, The University of Texas at Austin*

Mexico. Historians estimate the number of Mexicans at about 300,000, and some were US citizens. In one case, 88 Mexicans who were in the bed of a truck in temperatures over 110 degrees died. In addition, people harboring these individuals were subject to arrest, although companies hiring them faced no legal consequences. Estimates for a one-year period indicate about 20 percent were probably apprehended after being released because they crossed the border again. The program was discontinued in the mid-1960s.

Besides ongoing problems within its borders, tensions outside US borders continued. A number of worldwide conflicts tested Communist

Kids Count Too!

Governments use census information in many ways. The census gave immigration officials the figures they needed to determine quota numbers. Today, governments, businesses, and communities use census data to make decisions that affect us all.

YOU'LL NEED

* Paper, lined or unlined
* Pencil or pen
* Colored markers, pencils, or crayons (optional)
* Ruler
* Calculator (optional)

1. Make a copy of the Kids Count! map or use the map directly from the book. Or, you can trace the outline of the map and regions. Hawaii and Alaska are in the West region.

2. (Optional) Color all states in one region the same color; do not color over numbers. The dark lines show the borders for each region.

3. Make a table as shown to the right, using the ruler, pencil, and paper. You will need one empty row for each region, for a total of four.

4. Write the name of each region on a separate line in the first column.

5. Using the calculator or your brain, add up all the state kid populations for each region. (Completed tables and figures are on page 123.)

6. Write those numbers in the second column on the appropriate line.

7. Look at the map. How does your state compare to other states as far as its 1990 kid population?

8. What state has the highest kid population? What state has the lowest kid population?

9. What region do you live in? How does your region compare to others as far as its 1990 kid population?

10. What region has the smallest kid population? What region has the largest kid population?

11. How many regions have over three million kids? How many regions have fewer than five million kids?

12. When it comes to population, you count too!

| 1990 TOTAL US KID POPULATION BY REGION ||
Region	Total Kid Population by Region

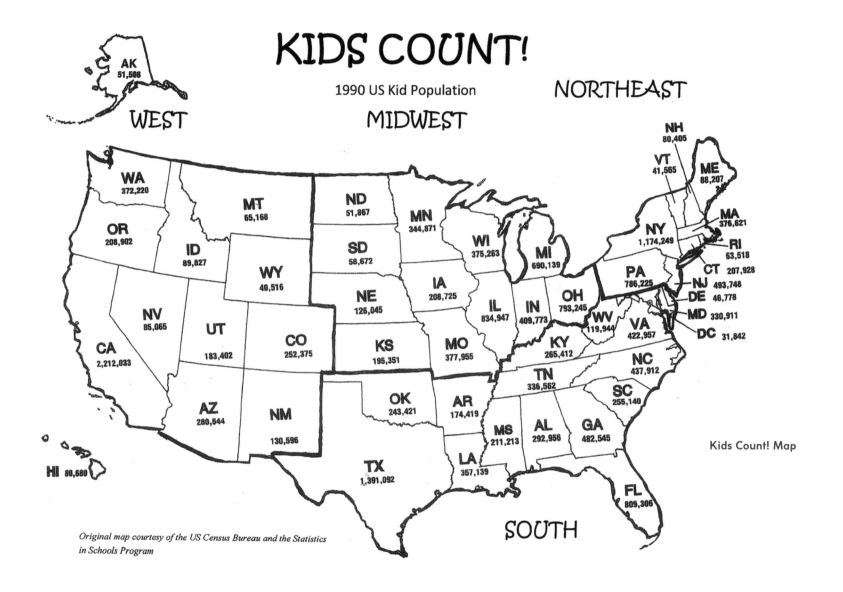

KIDS COUNT!

1990 US Kid Population

WEST

MIDWEST

NORTHEAST

SOUTH

AK 51,508

WA 372,220

OR 208,902

ID 89,827

MT 65,168

ND 51,867

MN 344,871

WI 375,263

MI 690,139

NH 80,405

VT 41,565

ME 88,207

NY 1,174,249

MA 376,621

RI 63,518

CT 207,928

PA 786,225

NJ 493,748

DE 46,778

MD 330,911

DC 31,842

NV 85,065

UT 183,402

WY 40,516

CO 252,375

NE 126,045

IA 208,725

IL 834,947

IN 409,773

OH 793,245

WV 119,944

VA 422,957

KY 265,412

CA 2,212,033

KS 195,351

MO 377,955

NC 437,912

TN 336,562

SC 255,140

AZ 280,544

NM 130,596

OK 243,421

AR 174,419

MS 211,213

AL 292,956

GA 482,545

HI 80,680

TX 1,391,092

LA 357,139

FL 809,306

Kids Count! Map

Original map courtesy of the US Census Bureau and the Statistics in Schools Program

aggression and the United States' image as leader of the free world. Uprisings in Hungary in 1956 pushed President Dwight D. Eisenhower to allow about 40,000 refugees into the United States. The US military provided much-needed medical aid, and navy ships transported thousands of desperate refugees. In spite of quota restrictions, about 320,000 immigrants entered the United States in the 1960s.

Europe and Asia were not the only places where immigrants faced displacement, persecution, and oppressive governments. Cuba, a US neighbor about 90 miles (145 km) off the Florida coast, added to tensions when its dictator, Fidel Castro, overthrew the former president in 1959. Cuba soon received support from the Soviet Union, and the revolution forced many people to flee.

President John F. Kennedy responded by signing the Migration and Refugee Assistance Act in 1962, providing aid to almost 2,000 refugees arriving weekly. Besides direct financial assistance and educational loans, this act helped resettle and care for children traveling alone to the United States. Other acts allowed Cuban relatives to join family members and gave those living in the United States more than two years to apply for permanent residency.

Laws during the 1950s and 1960s addressed issues such as immigrant spouses, fiancées, or children of American servicemen and servicewomen. Thousands of refugees escaping political unrest in countries like Czechoslovakia (now the Czech Republic and Slovakia) and Hong Kong added to the US ethnic mixture when they were admitted outside of quota restrictions. Over 90,000 engineers, doctors, and nurses worldwide, including from countries like Canada, South Africa, Japan, and Australia, moved to the United States during this period. This **brain drain** occurred in countries like Great Britain and Iran when well-educated people emigrated because of pull factors like higher standards of living and incomes.

In the following years, many people, including second- or third-generation Americans, found a new sense of pride in their heritage and the sacrifices their families had made. Some of this may be due in part to the civil rights movement, started in the 1950s, which pushed for equality for African Americans.

In a sweeping proclamation on May 11, 1965, President Lyndon B. Johnson made Ellis Island part of the Statue of Liberty National Monument under the control of the National Park Service. After Ellis Island's closure, the entire complex fell into disrepair. A decision to sell the property failed when the highest bid received was $200,000; the federal government had valued it at $6 million.

That same year, President Johnson signed the Immigration and Nationality Act of 1965 on October 3. Some elements of this law are still in effect. The number of immigrants was now limited to 20,000 people from any one country in the Eastern Hemisphere. The law eliminated the use of national origins to determine immigration numbers and leveled the playing field for countries like Turkey, North Korea, and India. Although the total number of immigrants allowed entry in any one year was 170,000, no limitations were placed on individual Western Hemisphere countries, with 120,000 total individuals permitted annually.

People from other parts of the world also began new lives in the United States. These included immigrants from Uganda, who left to escape a cruel dictator, and immigrants from Lebanon, who left because of a devastating civil war. But as horrible as steerage was centuries ago, one group arriving in the 1970s faced even riskier travel. And the response they received once they arrived was, for many, even worse.

A corrupt dictatorship in Haiti under François Duvalier, with a record of death and torture, forced thousands of Haitians to flee in the 1970s. Throughout the decade, an estimated 25,000 people left Haiti for the United States, with hundreds landing in Florida almost weekly. Risking their lives, people packed rickety boats, many almost to the point of sinking. Usually, the price of passage made the more than 700-mile voyage impossible. One Haitian said his trip with over 100 people in a 20-foot wooden sailboat cost $1,500.

Though refugees typically were received favorably, Haitians were believed to be here strictly for economic reasons. The United States defines an **asylum** seeker as someone who fears being persecuted based on religion, race, or political beliefs. According to US laws, no Haitians qualified for asylum status, even after many testified their lives were in danger if they returned. Religious and other groups interceded, but all Haitians were deported. The US Coast Guard turned boats away or towed them back before they reached shore.

President Lyndon B. Johnson makes remarks before signing the Immigration and Nationality Act in 1965.
Photo by Yoichi Okamoto. Courtesy of the LBJ Presidential Library

Many Haitian immigrants who were interviewed later denied being questioned about grounds for asylum, even though that was required. Advocates mostly blamed the US response on several factors: the United States was on friendly terms with Duvalier, and Haitians were Black, uneducated, and poor.

The end of the Vietnam War also affected immigration. With North Vietnam under Communist control, major operations helped thousands of Vietnamese emigrate to America. From 1975 to 1979, presidents Jimmy Carter and Gerald Ford used **parole** powers multiple times to bring 400,000 Vietnamese, Cambodians, and other

Let Your Voice Be Heard

One of the most important rights we have as US citizens is the right to vote. We elect people to represent us in government positions to enact laws and make decisions that affect everyone. For years, government decisions had an impact on the lives of natural-born citizens and immigrants alike.

How do government officials know how to vote? One way is to listen to their constituents—the people they represent. Think about immigration bills that have been passed because people voiced their opinions.

There are two senators and a number of representatives for every state. Each representative covers a particular area or district in his or her state. This is true of state officials as well. But they can't know how people feel about issues if we don't tell them. And you don't have to be of voting age to share your thoughts.

YOU'LL NEED

* Paper, lined or unlined
* Pencil or pen
* Internet access
* Envelope
* First-class stamp

1. Choose a local, state, or federal government official to write to. Issues differ depending on levels of government.

2. Focus on one major issue. Don't try to address several things in one letter. For example, are you interested in climate change, immigration, or education?

3. Do some research on the issue.

4. Explain in your letter why the issue is important to you.

5. Be specific about your thoughts without getting emotional. Don't use rude or impolite language. Be professional and spell out your concerns. A practice letter can help outline your thoughts.

6. If you're writing about a specific bill, use the official number of the legislation. Bills are assigned numbers in the order they are introduced in each session of Congress. Find information at congress.gov. State government websites are usually found at *statename*.gov.

7. Federal and state legislators are addressed as "The Honorable" followed by their full name in the address heading. When beginning your letter, you can say: Dear Senator (last name) or Dear Representative (last name).

8. Remember the three *P*s when reaching out: be professional, purposeful, and precise.

9. Try to keep your letter short. Legislators are busy; the more direct you are, the better.

10. Include your signature. Signed letters usually are more effective than unsigned ones.

11. Find the address for the elected official you chose at usa.gov. That site will direct you to state and local websites.

12. Write the official's address in the middle of the envelope. Include your return address in the upper left corner and a stamp in the upper right corner.

Southeast Asians to the United States. By 1985 that number was over 700,000. In 1978 an amended law removed the requirement for the number of immigrants from different hemispheres. The worldwide total now equaled the previous number of 290,000, with 20,000 immigrants or refugees allowed from each country as before.

Desperate People Use Desperate Measures

The United States responded to the Vietnam crisis with the Refugee Act in 1980. Although it allowed 50,000 people to apply as refugees, the total number annually decreased to 270,000. But this legislation legally acknowledged people seeking asylum, calling them **asylees**. This distinction allowed people already here—legally or illegally—to apply for asylum, limiting asylees to 5,000 per year.

Within 30 days of the act's signing, the United States faced its first test. Several men sought asylum at the Peruvian embassy in Cuba. When a guard was killed by one of the men, the Cuban government demanded their release to government custody, to await a trial. The Peruvian embassy refused. Shortly after, about 10,000 people sought protection at the embassy. Other embassies in Cuba offered to take in some of these people.

In a surprise move, Castro announced on April 20 that anyone wishing to emigrate to the United States could, but only if they went directly there and someone waited for them. The port of departure was Mariel, and almost 1,700 boats transported these "Marielitos." Some 125,000 people packed boats, often to the point of capsizing.

But this humanitarian response fueled anti-immigration fury when reports indicated that Castro had opened prisons and mental institutions to release unwanted Cubans. US refugee camps and prisons housed people until they were processed. Although some criminals were detained, most people were eventually released. The United States also took in an additional 25,000 Haitians. The Mariel boatlift ended in October 1980.

Immigration in an Ever-Changing World

—

"I want to let kids know that life as an immigrant is hard because you don't have the same benefits as Americans. I want to let the kids know that they are fortunate and they should be proud of [being] born here. Kids that are born here should be educated and take [ad]vantage of all [the] benefits."

—Adolfo Duarte, Guatemalan immigrant, 2013

Shortly after the Mariel boatlift, another historic event took place. The Statue of Liberty–Ellis Island Centennial Commission was established in 1982, partly to raise funds for the restoration of both national treasures. The projects raised about $350 million, of which over $150 million was used to restore Ellis Island. Renovated to look as it did from 1918 to 1924, Ellis Island reopened on September 9, 1990. But

Border with Mexico near Atascosa Trail. *Courtesy of Jean Kreyche*

the feelings of welcome that this historic building symbolized for so many people for so many years didn't necessarily carry over into the 20th century.

A Nation Moves Forward

In the 1980s, a movement pushing the "English-only" concept in schools took hold. Schools that taught in a particular foreign language were nothing new. Beginning in the 1830s, many schools with German students taught in their native language; most were church-affiliated. But many Americans saw this as an attempt by Germans to separate themselves ethnically and to avoid **assimilating** into American society. After the world wars, these feelings only increased.

The United States had never adopted an official language, but by 1911, a number of states voted that elementary classes be taught in English only. After World War I, this sentiment was reinforced when 21 states extended that condition to private schools. The US Supreme Court overruled that requirement.

Many people today pushing for English-only rules believe that one language unifies individuals as a nation. Some believe that if you live in the United States, you should adopt the language. Others opposed to the movement believe it separates people more than it unites them, and promotes ethnic or racial discrimination. In fact, after World War I, a US law made the use of the German language a criminal offense. This discrimination affected nonimmigrants too when American boarding schools forced Native American children to give up their language and their culture. And, of course, regardless of the language they spoke, African American children were segregated in schools from White students for years, as were Mexicans.

In the early 1900s, some cities created "**steamer classes**." These classes taught essential language skills to immigrant children as soon as they arrived in the United States. However, because these children were segregated from others and sometimes punished for speaking native languages, the classes were not always considered in their best interest.

Nowadays, many school districts offer **bilingual** or ESL—English as a Second Language—classes. Numerous studies note the positive effect for *all* students participating in dual language programs, including improving reading skills for even native English-speaking students, instilling more tolerant and welcoming attitudes toward others, and offering chances to experience cultural diversity.

With a number of languages spoken in the colonies, the Founding Fathers took no steps to make English the official language under the Constitution. They might have felt this move would potentially have divided people rather than unified them. However, 32 states have adopted English as their official language. Hawaii is the only state that recognizes two official languages—Hawaiian and English. Only Alaska recognizes more, with 20 **indigenous** languages along with English. When considering the push for English-only, it's worth noting that a US Census Bureau report indicated that from 2009 to 2013, people spoke 350 different languages throughout the country.

Congress Addresses Immigration Again

During a 10-year period from 1986 to 1996, Congress enacted three laws that addressed immigration or illegal immigration. The Immigration Reform and Control Act of 1986 was signed into law by President Ronald Reagan on November 6, 1986. To help control continuing illegal immigration, this law focused on employers, making it illegal for them to hire undocumented immigrants. This put the burden of documentation on employers. It also created a guest worker program for some seasonal workers in agriculture. Temporary legal status was granted to undocumented immigrants who arrived before January 1, 1982, if they resided in the United States continuously since that date. Anyone convicted of a felony or three or more misdemeanor crimes was ineligible.

Four years later, the Immigration Act of 1990 passed. Many people considered it the most comprehensive immigration bill since 1965. This legislation increased the number of immigrants allowed into the United States from 500,000 to 700,000. The law also allowed homosexual people and those positive with HIV (human immuno-deficiency virus).

A new **diversity immigrant** status allowed people from countries with less than 50,000 emigrants over the previous five years to be entered into a lottery for visas. Individuals randomly selected had to be high school graduates or have had two years of work experience. Those who obtained this visa entered the United States as permanent residents or with **green card** status and could live and work permanently in the country. No single country was allowed more than 7 percent of the total diversity visas available.

In 1991 President George W. Bush granted Deferred Enforced Departure status to Liberians in the United States. This program allowed a US president to grant this designation to **foreign nationals**. The program did not invite people outside the country to enter, but it removed the fear of deportation for people already in the country and gave them freedom to find work. As long as this status remained in place, these individuals could stay, although there were no processes in place for them to obtain US citizenship since this was a temporary order.

Undocumented immigrants again came to the government's attention with the signing of the Illegal Immigrant Reform and Immigrant Responsibility Act of 1996 on September 30. This bill addressed legal and illegal immigration issues. Much of it centered on six specific enforcement areas, including improvements to border control and addressing the smuggling of undocumented immigrants by "**coyotes**."

Another act signed by President Bill Clinton in 1996 made newly arriving immigrants ineligible to apply for welfare for a minimum of five years after arrival. States had the authority to enact their own welfare policies, and undocumented immigrants were and still are ineligible for food stamps and other public assistance.

A National Tragedy Leads to a Tougher Stance

Less than a week before the September 11, 2001, terrorist attacks on the World Trade Center in New York and the Pentagon in Washington, DC, President George W. Bush and Mexican president Vicente Fox had come to a tentative agreement on an immigration reform plan. This agreement addressed a new guest worker program for Mexican workers. It also would have granted temporary worker status to more than eight million undocumented immigrants in the United States. The plan favored increasing the number of green cards awarded each year.

But after 9/11, immigration actions focused on national security and terrorist threats. The government's response involved changes to several federal agencies and bureaus. On November 25, 2002, the Department of Homeland Security was created with broad oversight of other agencies and departments. In 2003 immigration fell under the control of US Citizenship and Immigration

Services (USCIS), previously the Bureau of Citizenship and Immigration Services.

USCIS deals with much of the administration and paperwork involved with immigration. US Immigration and Customs Enforcement handles federal law enforcement. Its agents investigate and address security issues with the country's transportation systems, bridges, power supplies, and borders. The US government also took steps to secure the nation's borders. Special tamper-proof visas allowed information sharing between agencies; enhanced technologies scanned and read visa information into data systems. But immigrants' rights organizations considered some programs simply a way to discriminate and to decrease immigration, particularly for poor or uneducated people.

Again in 2006, both the House of Representatives and the Senate each proposed an immigration reform bill addressing the estimated 10 to 11 million undocumented immigrants in the United States. Differences centered on specific terms, with the Senate version allowing **amnesty** to certain undocumented people depending on how long they had lived in America. With the end of the 109th Congress in January 2007, neither bill was enacted.

Executive Action Addresses Dreamers

On June 15, 2012, President Barack Obama announced an executive action that is still debated and challenged today. The Consideration of Deferred Action for Childhood Arrivals (DACA)

program allowed certain individuals brought here illegally as children to delay deportation or other actions leading to their removal from the United States. To qualify under DACA, a person had to be younger than 31 years old as of June 15, 2012, and brought to the country before age 16. The program granted people DACA status for two years and was renewable thereafter; participants were called Dreamers. While the program gave an estimated 690,000 Dreamers hope for a path to citizenship, that possibility depended, and still does depend, on government opposition or support.

On September 5, 2017, Donald Trump's administration ended the DACA program and stopped any new applicants. Those who already enrolled could continue until their current status expired. But several organizations challenged the action. The case made its way through several US district

Proimmigration supporters at a Washington, DC, rally, September 2017. *Shutterstock*

courts and eventually to the Supreme Court. On June 18, 2020, the Supreme Court ruled the Trump administration did not follow correct federal legal procedures to end the program and did not prove proper justification for its actions.

Despite this ruling, the Trump administration closed applications for DACA and lowered

Handwritten poster from the Women's March on Washington, 2017. *Courtesy of the Collection of the Smithsonian National Museum of African American History and Culture*

the renewal period to one year. In 2020 at least 140 major US companies—members of the Coalition for the American Dream—signed a letter supporting DACA. One of the first executive orders signed by President Joe Biden in January 2021 was the restoration of DACA for the millions of undocumented immigrants brought to the United States as minors.

Along with DACA was another program implemented by President Obama in 2014 called DAPA—Deferred Action for Parents of Americans and Lawful Permanent Residents. This executive order would have allowed undocumented parents of children born in the United States to apply for temporary status without fear of deportation under certain criteria. In addition, DACA would have been extended to people over 30 years old as long as they had come to the United States by age 16. Twenty-six states immediately challenged the DAPA order, and the case made its way to the Supreme Court. Only eight presiding justices served at the time because of the recent death of one member; the final vote was 4–4. Without support from a presidential administration or Congress, this order will not be implemented.

Temporary Protection Status (TPS) allowed people in the United States whose countries faced political upheaval; environmental disasters, such as earthquakes or floods; or other conditions that made it unsafe for them to return, to stay in the United States if their homeland was granted TPS protection. This allowed these individuals to live in the United States without fear of detention or deportation and granted them the right to work.

Currently, approximately 319,000 people from 12 countries live in the United States under TPS. Typically, TPS is given for 6-, 12-, or 18-month periods, but it may be renewed an indefinite number of times. Under the Biden administration, Secretary of Homeland Security Alejandra N. Mayorkas announced changes for a number of these countries. Many were granted TPS extensions through 2022 and 2023. Several countries are awaiting a court decision to overturn a ruling that attempted to end their protection status in 2020. People under TPS in the U.S. are not eligible for naturalization.

Physical Barriers and Detention

Physical structures have also been a controversial part of modern immigration enforcement, especially the roughly 1,950-mile Mexico–United States land border. Although portions of fences or walls had been built in 1909 by the United States and a small portion was erected by Mexico around 1918, more significant construction began around 1990. A 66-mile fence was built south of San Diego that extended into the Pacific Ocean. While undocumented crossings decreased there after construction, Arizona saw a 600 percent increase in crossings. Many of those crossings involved much more dangerous journeys through mountain and desert terrain. People paid coyotes to smuggle them into the country or took more risks to cross the border.

The Illegal Immigration Reform and Immigrant Responsibility Act of 1996 increased funding for Border Patrol efforts and funded a barrier

Diamondback rattlesnakes are just one danger faced when crossing the desert. *Courtesy of Jean Kreyche*

for a 14-mile area near San Diego. In addition, some landowners and ranchers built their own fences. Another effort was made to erect about 700 miles (1,126 km) of fencing along the border in 2007, but lawsuits by environmental and citizens groups ended construction. Environmental groups argued against the fence's impact on endangered animals and clean water protections. Arizona's Tohono O'odham Nation also objected to fencing on its reservation because the project received no input from tribal leaders. In addition, tribal members, who live on each side of the border, would be unable to cross freely with a barrier in place.

A bill passed in 2007 allowed for a protection system that uses modern technology such as cameras, laser radar, and other surveillance equipment to patrol sections of the border. But some nearby landowners complained about privacy and safety issues. Virtual walls have been used along the almost 4,000-mile Canada–United States border

ANSWERING THE CALL TO HUMANITY

Two groups addressing the issue of humanitarian aid to migrants in the desert in Arizona are Humane Borders and Tucson Samaritans, or *Los Samaritanos*. Both groups are composed of volunteers.

Humane Borders maintains water stations throughout the Sonoran Desert, marked by blue flags on long poles visible from a distance. Some people who oppose this aid shoot holes in the water tanks or jugs or try to empty them. Tucson Samaritans use four-wheel-drive vehicles to reach more remote areas in search of people who need food, emergency medical care, and water.

Many volunteers speak fluent Spanish and, especially for the Tucson Samaritans, include doctors, nurses, and people with wilderness training. Both groups follow legal procedures, including not transporting people. If migrants wish to turn themselves in, volunteers call Border Patrol.

Humane Border also documents migrant deaths and maintains a migrant death map (https://humaneborders.info). This allows family members, volunteers, and others to access the map on the website, which includes the identities of deceased individuals when that information is known. Information comes from the county medical examiner's office.

Whenever remains are found by either group, volunteers call local law enforcement authorities, including the sheriff, park rangers, or Border Patrol agents. Remains are sent to or picked up by the office of the county medical examiner.

Typically, when they encounter someone, Samaritan volunteers ask a list of six questions to determine the severity of the situation:

1. How old are you?
2. How many days were you in the desert?
3. How much water did you carry?
4. When was the last time you urinated?
5. Do you hurt anywhere?
6. Do you have any other illnesses (diabetes or other health issues)?

Both groups also attempt to bring attention to the situation of undocumented people and to work with government officials to address legislation.

Mike Kreyche, a member of the Tucscon Samaritans who maintains the migrant death map for Humane Borders, writes a note before leaving water in the desert. *Photo by Jean Kreyche*

since shortly after 9/11. This border enforcement method uses solar-powered towers to detect movement across the border, in some cases with 97 percent accuracy, and sends data directly to Border Patrol cell phones. In 2020 a private company was contracted to erect towers using computer technology and imagery to monitor physical movement near the border. A private group has also constructed an 18-foot wall on a roughly half-mile section of the US southwestern border, which they believe is more efficient and less expensive than government efforts.

Detention centers throughout the United States were previously run by the US government at ports like Ellis Island and Angel Island. Today, 70 percent of them are managed by private companies that contract with the government. Advocates for immigration have long complained about the horrible living conditions at these facilities. Another complaint involves the cost, which reports have estimated to be $127 to as high as $775 per day for the care of one detainee. Just like during processing at Ellis Island, the majority of these people are awaiting hearings on the status of their immigration applications. They are seeking asylum status or legal entry into the United States. While the average wait time is four weeks, some people have been in detention for years.

US Policy and Minors

Push factors have increased the number of asylees and refugees desperate for safety. Particularly during the Obama administration, there was a huge

Border Patrol checkpoint 25 miles (40.2 km) north of the Mexico–United States border. *Courtesy of Jean Kreyche*

spike in immigrants appearing at the Mexico–United States border. Even more striking was the number of minors who appeared, often alone. Immigration supporters pushed the government to allow these children an opportunity to present their need for asylum in court. Opponents of immigration blamed the situation on the individuals themselves.

About one-third of the children arriving at the southwestern border in 2014 came from Honduras, where one city—San Pedro Sula—is considered the murder capital of the world. Gang violence is an ongoing issue throughout Central America. By September 2019, approximately 76,000 minors were apprehended by US authorities at the Mexico–United States border, with just over 40,000 more stopped in Mexico. According to Customs and Border Protection, this represents an increase of about 52 percent during the last **fiscal year**.

TWO IMMIGRANTS, TWO STORIES

At 13 years old, Adolfo Duarte said goodbye to his family and friends in Guatemala. He spoke no English, but his family supported the dangerous journey he faced alone. Thanks to a generous uncle and some kind strangers, Duarte made it to Mexico. He and others crossed the Rio Grande River in a small boat to Hidalgo, Texas, where he applied for Special Immigrant Juvenile Status.

Duarte remembers the frightening trip, particularly in Mexico where he knew the dangers of being robbed or worse. But he appreciates the chance at a better life, even though he gets the flu every winter!

Adolfo Duarte on his first day of flight school. *Courtesy of Santos Lemus*

Since he arrived, Duarte has since finished middle and high school and earned an associate's degree in science while working in a restaurant. His goal to become a pilot was disrupted by the COVID-19 pandemic, but he hopes eventually to achieve that dream. It took Duarte two years to get a green card, and on April 9, 2021, after satisfying the five-year residency requirement, he received his certificate of naturalization and is eligible to vote in the next election.

Noman Biswas began hearing the words *United States* when he was about five years old. His family waited 12 years for approval to come to the United States and received their green cards shortly after they arrived. Biswas's uncle sponsored the family—Biswas, his parents, and his younger brother.

At 17, Biswas entered public school at the end of 10th grade, although he was a senior in his home country of Bangladesh. Speaking little English when he arrived in the United States, he was fortunate to take ESL classes. Playing soccer also helped his language skills, but he did not graduate with his classmates because of graduation requirements. At 24, he has passed all but one class for the equivalency of a high school diploma. He has taken and passed his citizenship exam and looks forward to voting in his first election in 2022. Currently working in a pharmacy, Biswas plans to attend community college before applying to the the police academy.

Noman Biswas at the pharmacy where he works. *Courtesy of Noman Biswas*

One provision today affecting minors is Special Immigrant Juvenile Status, which covers minors who are undocumented and have dealt with abuse, abandonment, or neglect by one or both parents. Abandonment applies to children who arrive in the United States without parents. There are a number of stipulations, including being under 21 years old and unmarried, but these individuals eventually have a path to naturalization.

Despite worldwide criticism, the Trump administration's zero tolerance policy led to thousands of children being separated from their families and held in detention centers across the country. Some are still there today. A federal judge ordered the end to family separations in June 2018, which allowed 2,800 families to be reunited. But in January 2020, that same judge allowed exceptions to this policy if it was in the best interest of the child, such as parents deemed unfit or a danger to a child. This included parents with health issues or a criminal history, which could include a traffic ticket. Numerous reports have addressed issues of abuse, unsanitary conditions, and concerns about the health and safety of children in detention. The Biden administration has established a task force to take on the difficult job of reuniting separated families, either in their country of origin or in the United States.

Immigration in a Changing World

It's difficult to understand the complexity of immigration today without looking at current numbers. In spite of laws from 2000 to 2020 that increased deportations and affected immigrants, immigration numbers have climbed into the 21st century. According to a survey by the US Census Bureau, the immigrant population in the United States reached 44.7 million total legal and undocumented immigrants as of 2018. Also as of that year, 13.7 percent of the total population of the United States were immigrants, lower than the highest percentage of 14.7 in 1910. From 2010 to 2018, the United States has seen an increase in immigrants from countries like Venezuela, the Dominican Republic, and Cuba. The largest drop in any one year during that period was for immigrants from Mexico, with about 500,000 fewer arriving in 2018.

Besides the hundreds of thousands of descendants of formerly enslaved people living in the United States, it's also important to recognize Black immigrants. Although Black immigrants have come to this country for centuries, one notable period was from 1910 to 1930, when large numbers arrived from the West Indies. Many African Americans, particularly from the South, settled in New York in an area known as Harlem. With the growth of art, music, finances, and businesses in this area, the period from 1910 to the mid-1930s became known as the Harlem Renaissance. Many people consider this the "golden age" of Black and African American culture, noting the achievements of numerous Black artists, writers, singers, entrepreneurs, and civic leaders.

In 1980 there were about 816,000 Black immigrants living in the US. By 2016 that number had increased to about 4.2 million. African immigrants came from countries like Nigeria, Ghana,

Sponsor an International Picnic

Spending time with people from other cultures is the best way to learn about their customs and traditions. And one thing that connects people is sharing food. June 18 is International Picnic Day, but you can choose any day you want for your picnic. You'll need to talk to your parents or another adult to do this activity.

YOU'LL NEED

* Unlined paper
* Pencil or pen
* Colored markers, pencils, or crayons
* Craft supplies (optional)
* Outdoor furniture, like chairs and tables
* Disposable tableware, like paper plates, plastic cups, and plastic forks and knives
* Food that reflects your ancestry or culture

1. Check with your parents or other adult about using a local park, your driveway, yard, or garage for your picnic.

2. Create flyers giving the name, date, time, and location of your event.

3. Explain what the picnic is about and suggest people bring at least one dish or other food that reflects their culture.

4. Share flyers with classmates, neighbors, or church members.

5. With your parents or other adult, plan food to serve that reflects your family's ancestry or culture.

6. Set up your picnic space by arranging the chairs and setting the tables with the tableware.

7. Buy or prepare your food and help arriving guests arrange food in one location. Keep in mind issues like weather and food safety, depending on the temperature.

8. Enjoy the day! You could also talk to your teacher about having an international day in your classroom. Everyone can bring food to share that reflects their ancestry or culture.

Kenya, Ethiopia, and Somalia. But the majority of these new immigrants—almost 1.4 million—came from Jamaica and Haiti.

About 15 percent are undocumented, but almost 60 percent of foreign-born Black immigrants are US citizens. Recently, the number of Black people seeking entry at the Mexico–United States border more than doubled, from 2,700 in 2018 to about 5,800 in 2019. These new arrivals are not only from the Caribbean but also from Africa. Besides the challenges of traveling to Mexico, they report facing abuse and discrimination along the way.

One law, established on February 24, 2020, applied to people seeking legal visas and green cards and was similar to some immigration laws implemented much earlier at Ellis Island. In this case, a person applying for permanent resident status through a family petition may be ineligible if it's determined the person is likely to rely on government benefits in the future.

Although the Trump administration put into place about 400 executive actions affecting immigration, the latest data suggests that changes in immigration were not significantly different than in previous periods throughout US history. What did have a profound impact were the effects of the COVID-19 pandemic. While approximately 459,000 immigrant visas to the US were awarded in fiscal year 2019, that number dropped to slightly more than 250,000 for fiscal year 2020. Most of this decrease is believed to be because of the closure of US consulates due to the pandemic. For the first half of 2020, global migration numbers dropped by about 50 percent.

According to data from the Pew Research Center, the Biden administration is looking to increase the number of refugees admitted to the US and the number of visas awarded to immigrants seeking legal residency in the future. The administration also plans to streamline the processing of immigrants with family members already in the country. This would help to simplify the application system and clear up some of the backlog of applications for people who have been waiting years for decisions to be made.

For people in favor of decreasing the number of immigrants—both documented and undocumented—these proposals may not come as welcome news. But for others, who support immigration reform and look at the impact of immigration on the US labor market, these numbers will have important consequences. Two economists for the Federal Reserve Board noted that immigrants and their children added over 50 percent to the growth in worker numbers in the United States in the last 20 years. Decreasing immigration numbers, should they become reality, could slow US recovery from issues like the COVID-19 pandemic.

There is one thing worth thinking about with the Trump administration's push to decrease immigration and tighten the borders. People who typically feed Americans, meaning those working on dairy farms and in orchards, fields, and food-packing facilities, are often undocumented immigrants, though others work under a seasonal guest worker program. Undocumented workers live with the fear that at any time they could be detained and deported, even though many have lived and raised families in the United States for years.

During the outbreak of the COVID-19 pandemic in early 2020, these workers could carry a letter from their US employers indicating that the DHS considered them "critical to the food supply." They could not be found in violation of state or local stay-at-home orders. But that did not protect them from detention and deportation. They also faced increased risk of contracting the coronavirus, as have all essential workers.

The Biden administration also supports changes that will benefit immigrant farmworkers, including rules that address working conditions and that might ultimately open the way to citizenship.

What Does the Future Hold for Immigration?

People have strong viewpoints on both sides of the immigration issue. Going forward, this is likely to continue. If the last 200-plus years are any example, there will be no easy answers to future legislation. While President Joe Biden has proposed a plan that includes a path to citizenship for *all* undocumented individuals in the United States—some 11 million people—the future remains uncertain for those individuals.

For hundreds of years, immigrants have contributed to the culture and success of the United States. Their food, holiday traditions, and religious practices have all added to the rich and colorful history of an ever-changing America. Immigrants have advanced new ideas, creative solutions to existing problems, and improvements in technology. Many have founded businesses that employ thousands of people. A country that embraces a spirit of community and tolerates differing opinions lets everyone live full and productive lives.

So what role can *you* play? There are plenty of books and information available online about the subject if you want to learn more. Just google *immigration* and see what comes up.

Talk to your friends and classmates about the immigration issue. If there are students in your school or community who have different ethnicity than you—whether they are first-generation Americans or not, documented or undocumented—reach out to them. Most people, kids included, like to talk about themselves. But be respectful of their feelings, especially issues they don't want to discuss.

Even though you may have strong feelings about the issue of immigration, you can never have too much information. The more you learn, the more informed you'll be!

Make an Immigration Time Line

A time line helps historians, educators, and others see the history of events. It can show historical events or dates within a particular time frame, like the Civil War. A time line has a beginning and an end and can span centuries or a single year.

YOU'LL NEED

❋ Paper, lined or unlined

❋ Pencil or pen

❋ Ruler

1. Draw or photocopy the time line and table on this page or use the ones in the book.

2. How many evenly spaced time periods are there from beginning to end?

3. What time span does each dot on the line represent—one year, one decade, or some other combination, like a 30-year period?

4. Write the correct year under each dot on the line.

5. Find each historical event listed in the table to the right in this book. Write the date next to the correct event.

6. For each event, find its *approximate* place on the time line and mark it with a dot. You will have to estimate where on the time line an event occurred. Write the correct year under the mark.

7. Extend vertical lines up from each of the dots you added to the time line and write the event that each dot corresponds to on these lines. (The completed time line is on page 123.)

Historical Event	Year
Ellis Island opened	
Foreign Miners' License Act enacted	
Draft Riot	
Angel Island opened	
Haymarket Square Riot	
Record arrivals at Ellis Island	
Japanese internment begins	
California passes laws against Chinese	
Border Patrol established	
Anti-Vagrancy Act passed	

1850 ●━━●━━●━━●━━●━━●━━●━━●━━●━━●━━●━━● 1950

GLOSSARY

amnesty An official pardon, usually to a large group of people and often for political reasons

anarchists People who resist authority, especially that of an established government

asylees People seeking asylum protections

asylum Protection granted to someone who fears being persecuted based on religion, race, or political beliefs

ballast Gravel, sand, iron, or other material placed in the lower part of a vessel to improve stability

berth A fixed bunk or bed on a ship, train, or other mode of transportation

bilingual Being able to use two languages

bond A monetary guarantee provided by someone that an immigrant would not become a public charge

brain drain Emigration of highly skilled and professional people from one country to another

chain migration Process by which green card holders or legal residents sponsor a family member to emigrate

coyotes People who smuggle others across the US border, usually for a high fee

deport To force someone to leave a country

deportation The act of removing someone from a country

detainees People who are held in custody, often for political reasons

disembark To leave a ship to go ashore

displaced persons People forced to leave their country because of war or a natural disaster

diversity immigrants People randomly selected for green card status in the United States

embark To board a ship

emigration The act of leaving a country to settle elsewhere

ethnicity The sharing of a common culture, nationality, language, or religion

fiscal year A one-year period, not necessarily beginning on January 1, that a government, business, or organization uses to typically record budgeting information and other data

foreign nationals People who are not naturalized citizens in the country where they live

green card An identification card allowing a person to legally live and work in the United States

immigrants People who travel to another country to take up permanent residence

immigration The process of coming to live permanently in another country

indentured servants People bound to work for others for a specific period of time in exchange for passage or upkeep

indigenous Native to a particular region or country

mandatorily excludable Denied entry by law without any options

manifest A list of passengers that includes specific information

migration The process of moving from one place to another

money changers People who exchanged money from one country's currency to another's

nativism A policy of favoring native inhabitants as opposed to immigrants

naturalization The process to admit a foreign-born person as a citizen of another country

paper sons / paper daughters People who purchase false papers showing they are the son or daughter of a US citizen

parole The option for the president or other governmental agencies, such as the Department of Homeland Security, to temporarily allow certain noncitizens to enter the United States

pull factors Usually positive issues within another country that encourage people to relocate there

push factors Usually negative factors within a county that encourage people to leave

quota A fixed number of people needed (for the draft); the number of people, especially from one country, allowed to enter the United States (for immigrants)

quarantine To isolate or separate from others, particularly because of infectious diseases

redemptioners Immigrants who sell their services for a specific period of time in return for passage to America

refugee camp A temporary shelter that offers assistance and protection for people who leave a country due to war, violence, or conflict

refugees People who leave a country due to war, violence, or conflict, or because of religious or political beliefs

repatriate To return someone to his or her country of origin

repatriation drives Government raids targeting specific populations with the intent to return people to their country of origin

restrictionists People who support limitations on US immigration

segregation The act of separating people or isolating people from others, usually because of race

special board of inquiry Board set up to investigate specific issues of immigration, particularly regarding deportation

steamer classes Classes set up in the early 1900s to integrate immigrant children and teach English

steerage Ship accommodations found below deck, in an area that also served as the cargo hold; mostly occupied by lower class travelers

undocumented immigrants Foreign-born people with no legal status in a country

visa An endorsement in a passport that allows someone to enter, leave, or stay in a country for an extended period of time

ANSWERS REVEALED

Could You Survive?

TOTAL WEEKLY WAGES (Daily amounts multiplied by 6)	
Unskilled factory worker	$6.36/week
General laborer	$8.04/week
Miner	$8.76/week
Coal heaver	$8.10/week

RENT (Monthly amounts divided by 4)	
Four-room tenement	$2.40/week
Six-room tenement	$2.95/week

Make Your Money Count

Item	Price in US $	Country	Amount of foreign currency needed
Watch	$125	Canada	156.61 CAD
Scarf	$23	Italy	19.50 EUR
Book	$16	Tanzania	36,992.16 TZS
Hat	$49	Mexico	978.82 MXN
Chocolate	$32	Switzerland	29.14 CHF
Painting	$75	Japan	8,250.75 JPY
Shoes	$189	Bangladesh	15,746.44 BDT
Jacket	$147	India	10,879.12 INR

Matching and Creating Medical Letters

B	Back
C	Conjunctivitis (eye infection)
Ct	Trachoma (eye infection)
E	Eyes
F	Face
Ft	Feet
G	Goiter (enlarged thyroid)
H	Heart
K	Hernia
L	Lameness
N	Neck
P	Physical and lungs
Pg	Pregnancy
Sc	Scalp
S	Senility
X	Suspected mental defect
(X)	Definite sign of mental defect observed

Kids Count Too!

1990 TOTAL US KID POPULATION BY REGION	
Region	Total Kid Population by Region
West	4,052,836
Midwest	4,466,853
South	6,209,549
Northeast	3,312,466

What state has the highest kid population? **California**
What state has the lowest kid population? **Delaware**
What region has the smallest kid population? **Northeast**
What region has the largest kid population? **South**
How many regions have over three million kids? **Four**
How many regions have fewer than five million kids? **Three**

How Did Ethnicity Change?

IMMIGRATION TO THE UNITED STATES BY DECADE				
	1880-1889	1890-1899	1900-1909	1910-1919
	TOTAL	TOTAL	TOTAL	TOTAL
Northwestern Europe	72.3	49.4	21.6	17.5
Central Europe	6.8	17.4	24.8	18.6
Southeastern Europe	9.1	30.5	46.2	43.3
Asia	1.3	1.5	2.9	3.1
Central and South America	9.9	1.1	3.4	16.9
Other countries	0.2	0.5	0.6	0.5

Make an Immigration Time Line

TIME LINE COMPLETED

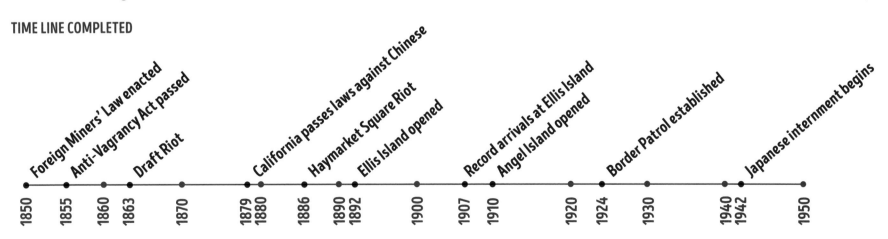

WEBSITES AND PLACES TO VISIT

Angel Island Immigration Station

Access to the island is by private boat or public ferry from San Francisco or Tiburon. For information on tours, hours, or admission, call (415) 435-5390 or visit the website.

https://www.aiisf.org/visit

Border Patrol Museum

4315 Woodrow Bean Trans Mt. Rd., El Paso, TX 79924

1-877-276-8738 (toll-free)

https://www.borderpatrolmuseum.com/

Chinese American Museum of Chicago

238 West 23rd St., Chicago, IL 60616

312-949-1000

https://ccamuseum.org/

Ellis Island

Access is to the island is by ferry through Statue Cruises, LLC. For tickets, call 1-877-LADY-TIX or 201-604-2800 or visit the website.

https://www.statueofliberty.org/ellis-island/national-immigration-museum/

El Museo del Barrio

1230 Fifth Ave. at 104th St., New York, NY 10029

212-831-7272

https://www.elmuseo.org/about/

Immigration Museum

400 Flinders St., Melbourne, Victoria, 3000 (Australia)

+61 3 8341 7777 (outside Australia) or 13 11 02 (general)

https://museumsvictoria.com.au/immigrationmuseum

Migration Museum

Lewisham Shopping Centre (entrance in Central Square), Unit 11, London SE13 7HB

(email) info@migrationmuseum.org

https://www.migrationmuseum.org/

Museum at Eldridge Street

12 Eldridge St., New York, NY 10002

212-219-0302

https://www.eldridgestreet.org/

Museum of Chinese in America

215 Centre St., New York, NY 10013

855-055-MOCA

https://www.mocanyc.org/

Plimoth-Patuxet Museums

137 Warren Ave., Plymouth, MA 02360

508-746-1622

https://www.plimoth.org/

Safe Haven Holocaust Refugee Shelter Museum

2 East 7th St., Oswego, NY 13126

315-342-3003

https://www.safehavenmuseum.com/

Statue of Liberty

Access is to the island is by ferry through Statue Cruises, LLC.

For tickets, call 1-877-LADY-TIX or 201-604-2800 or visit the website.

https://www.nps.gov/stli/index.htm

Tenement Museum

103 Orchard St., New York, NY 10002

1-877-975-3786

https://www.tenement.org/

US Holocaust Memorial Museum

100 Raoul Wallenberg Place, SW, Washington, DC 20024-2126

202-488-0400

https://www.ushmm.org/

NOTES

---

1. Castle Island: The Foundation for Ellis Island

"Dear Sister, do": William I. Thomas and Florian Znaniecki, *The Polish Peasant in Europe* and *America: Monograph of an Immigrant Group*, accessed May 13, 2020, https://www.jaha.org/edu/discovery_center /push-pull/letterstohome.html.

"a scandal and": Dennis Wepman, *Immigration: From the Founding of Virginia to the Closing of Ellis Island* (New York: Facts on File, 2002), 206.

2. Ellis Island: A New Gateway to America

"The word 'America'": Wilton S. Tifft, *Ellis Island* (Chicago: Contemporary Books, 1990), flyleaf.

"idiots, insane persons,": Vincent I. Cannato, *American Passage: The History of Ellis Island* (New York: HarperCollins, 2009), 52.

"the doctors made": Dr. Howard Markel, "Before Ebola, Ellis Island's Terrifying Medical Inspections," accessed May 10, 2020.

"mandatorily excludable": Peter Morton Goan, *Ellis Island Interviews* (New York: Fall River Press, 1997), 3.

3. Ellis Island: Island of Tears, Island of Joy

"Immigration officials slammed": Goan, *Ellis Island Interviews*, 124.

"Many immigrants had": Martin W. Sandler, *Immigrants* (New York: HarperCollins Publishers, 1995), 18.

"I was powerless": Dorothy and Thomas Hoobler, *We Are Americans: Voices of the Immigration Experience* (New York: Scholastic, 2003), 27.

4. When It All Began

"After we had": Hoobler and Hoobler, *We Are Americans*, 27.

"begging . . . pretending that": Wepman, *Immigration*, 42.

5. A Great Migration Begins

"[A] crowded immigrant": Wepman, *Immigration*, 122.

"any alien, being": Wepman, 69.

6. A New Country Confronts New Changes

"It was a": Wepman, *Immigration,* 155.

"a rich man's": Connie Golding, Ford's Theatre blog, *Civil War 150: A Rich Man's War and a Poor Man's Fight,* accessed June 11, 2020, https://www.fords.org/blog/post/civil-war-150-a-rich-mans-war-and-a-poor-mans-fight/.

"all persons born": Legal Information Institute, Cornell Law School, *14th Amendment,* accessed June 15, 2020, https://www.law.cornell.edu/constitution/amendmentxiv.

"New York's most": National Park Service, *Jacob Riis Biography,* accessed May 9, 2020, https://www.nps.gov/gate/learn/historyculture/jacob-riis-biography.htm.

7. Immigration Changes the United States Forever

"Nearly any hour": Wepman, *Immigration,* 233.

"San Francisco is": Wepman, 214.

8. World Crises and the US Response

"I wanted to": Wepman, *Immigration,* 273.

"American Jobs for": Becky Little, "The U.S. Deported a Million of its Own Citizens to Mexico During the Great Depression," accessed July 4, 2020, https://www.history.com/news/great-depression-repatriation-drives-mexico-deportation.

"That is the tragedy": Melissa Block, All Things Considered, "Remembering California's 'Repatriation Program,'" accessed July 6, 2020, https://www.npr.org/templates/story/story.php?storyId=5079627.

9. The United States Confronts Global Issues Again

"Nowadays, sometimes I": Wepman, *Immigration,* 324.

"visas should be": "Words of Peace, Words of War," *New York Times,* December 22, 1945.

"It is with": Harry S. Truman Library, "Statement by the President Upon Signing the Displaced Persons Act," accessed July 8, 2020, https://www.trumanlibrary.gov/library/public-papers/142/statement-president-upon-signing-displaced-persons-act.

"The greatest vice": Wepman, *Immigration,* 279.

10. Immigration in an Ever-Changing World

"I want to": Adolfo Duarte, e-mail interview, June 19, 2020.

"critical to the": Miriam Jordan, "Farmworkers Mostly Undocumented, Become 'Essential' During Pandemic," *New York Times,* https://www.nytimes.com/2020/04/02/us/coronavirus-undocumented-immigrant-farmworkers-agriculture.html.

SELECTED BIBLIOGRAPHY

———

*Books suitable for children

*Bial, Raymond. *Ellis Island*. New York: Houghton Mifflin Books for Children, 2009.

*Brundle, Harriet. *Immigration*. King's Lynn, Norfolk: Book Life, 2017.

*Burgan, Michael. *Ellis Island*. North Mankato, MN: Capstone Press, 2014.

Cannato, Vincent I. *American Passage*. New York: HarperCollins, 2009.

Daniels, Roger. *Coming to America*. New York: HarperCollins Publishers, 2002.

*Freedman, Russell. *Immigrant Kids*. New York: Puffin Books, 1995.

Goan, Peter Morton. *Ellis Island Interviews*. New York: Fall River Press, 1997.

*Hicks, Terry Allan. *Ellis Island*. Tarrytown, NY: Marshall Cavendish Benchmark, 2007.

Hoobler, Dorothy and Thomas. *We Are Americans: Voices of the Immigration Experience*. New York: Scholastic, 2003.

*Hopkins, Deborah. *Shutting Out the Sky*. New York: Orchard Books, 2003.

*Jacobs, William Jay. *Ellis Island*. New York: Charles Scribner's Sons, 1990.

*Kenney, Karen Latchana. *Ellis Island*. Edina, MN: Magic Wagon, 2011.

Klapper, Melissa R. *Small Strangers*. Chicago: Ivan R. Dee, 2017.

Lawler, Veronica. *I Was Dreaming to Come to America*. New York: Viking, 1995.

Lee, Erika, and Judy Yung. *Angel Island*. New York: Oxford University Press, 2020.

Riis, Jacob. *How the Other Half Lives*. Mansfield Centre, CT: Martino Publishing, 2015. Originally published by Scribner's in 1890.

*Sandler, Martin W. *Immigrants*. New York: HarperCollins Publishers, 1995.

*Sandler, Martin W. *Island of Hope*. New York: Scholastic Nonfiction, 2004.

*Swain, Gwenyth. *Hope and Tears*. Honesdale, PA: Calkins Creek, 2012.

Thomas, William L., and Florian Znaniecki. *The Polish Peasant in Europe and America*. Boston: The Gorham Press, 1918.

Tifft, Wilton S. *Ellis Island*. Chicago: Contemporary Books, 1990.

Wepman, Dennis. *Immigration*. New York: Facts on File, 2002.

*Woodruff, Elvira. *The Orphan of Ellis Island*. New York: Scholastic Press, 1997.

INDEX

Page numbers in italics refer to illustrations and captions.

abandonment, 115
Act to Encourage Immigration (1864), 61
activities
    cooking, 19, 116
    craft, 43, 51, 55, 68, 91, 116
    math, 8–9, 32–33
    research, 3, 51, 73, 77, 86–87, 98–99, 119
    science, 38, 64–65
    writing, 6, 14, 27, 102
Adams, John, 49
Adams, Samuel, 68
Alien Contract Labor Law of 1885, 29
alien enemies, 49, 82–83, 90, 91
Alien Enemies Act of 1798, 49, 82
American Eugenics Society, 66
amnesty programs, 109
anarchists, 66, 83, 96
Andersson, Brian, 13
Angel Island, 75–76, *75*, 78, 82, 89
Angels Camp, California, *46*
anti-immigration sentiments, 50, 52, 65–67, 84, 90, 97, 103, 106–107

Anti-Vagrancy Act of 1855, 56
assimilation, 106
asylum seekers (asylees), 101, 103, 113
A-TEAM (Athletes in Temporary Employment as Agricultural Manpower), 88
Ayllón, Lucas Vázquez de, 41

baggage handling, 5–6, 25
Batton, Gary, 53
Bedloe's Island, 11
Beringia, *36–37, 37*, 38
Biden, Joe, 110, 115, 117, 118
bilingualism, 107
Binet, Alfred, 79
Binet test, 79
birds of passage, 7
Biswas, Noman, 114, *114*
Black immigrants, 76, 115, 117
Black Indians, 41
border enforcement methods, 111, 113
Border Patrol, 85, 97
Bracero Program, 88, 89–90
brain drain, 100
British Passenger Act of 1803, 50
Bureau of Immigration, 9, 88

Bureau of Naturalization, 88
Bush, George W., 108
buttonhooks, *26*

Californios, 56
Canada, immigration through, 50, 67, 69, 85
Canada–United States border, 111, 113
Carriage of Passengers Act of 1855, 5
Carter, Jimmy, 101
Castle Clinton National Monument, 5
Castle Garden, *xii*, 5–6, *7*, 9
Castro, Fidel, 100, 103
Central Pacific Railroad, 62
chain migration, 50, 96
Chavez, Cesar, 88
Chenitz, Rachel, 26
children. *See also* DACA program; paper sons and daughters
    deportation of, 30
    education of, 74, 107
    at Ellis Island, *16, 30*
    employment of, *70*, 74–75, *74*, 89
    Fourteenth Amendment and, 62
    medical examination of, 28

new roles assumed by, 72, 74–75
separation from family, 18, 115
traveling alone, 72, 100, 113
Chinese Exclusion Act (1882), 63, 90
Chinese immigrants, 54, 56–57, *58*, 62–63, *63*, 75–78, 85, 90
Chinese poetic verse, *76*
Choctaw nation, 53
cholera outbreak, 13, 15
citizenship, paths to, 49, 60, 82, 109, 117–118
Citizenship and Immigration Services (USCIS), 108–109
Civil War Military Draft Act, 61
Cleveland, Grover, 9, 69
Clinton, Bill, 108
coaching books, 78
Coalition for the American Dream, 110
Colpo, Theresa (Bertuzzi), Jean, and John, *29*
Common Sense (Paine), 48
Communism, fear of, 83, 96
Confederate Draft Act (1862), 60
Conscription Act, 61
Consideration of Deferred Action for Child-hood Arrivals. *See* DACA program
COVID-19 pandemic, 15, 117–118
Cox, Delton, 53
coyotes. *See* smugglers and smuggling, of immigrants
Cuban refugees, *92*, 100, 103
Curran, Henry, 31

DACA program, 109–110
DAPA program, 110
Dare, Virginia, 37
Dawson, Scott, 39
Declaration of Independence, immigrant signers of, 49
DeCrescenzo, Luciano, 24
Deferred Action for Childhood Arrivals (DACA). *See* DACA program

Deferred Action for Parents of Americans and Lawful Permanent Residents (DAPA). *See* DAPA program
Deferred Enforced Departure (DED), 108
Department of Homeland Security (DHS), 108
deportations, 24, 28–31, 83, 88, 97
detention and detainees, 17, 25, 31, 75–76, 83, 111
detention centers, 82, 91, 113
Diary of Anne Frank, The (Frank), 95
discrimination, 62–63, *63*, 65–66, 75–76, *97*, 107
Displaced Persons Act (1948), 94–95
displaced persons (DPs), 94, 96
diversity immigrant status, 108
draft acts, 60–61
draft riots. *See* New York City Draft Riots
Dreamers, 109–110
Duarte, Adolfo, 114, *114*
Dunn, Joseph, 87, 88
Dutch explorations, 42, 44
Duvalier, François, 101

Eisenhower, Dwight D., 100
El Dorado (shrimp boat), *92*
Ellis, Samuel, 12
Ellis Island, 11–31
closing of, 96
construction of, 12
first arrivals at, 13
name changes at, *33*
photographs taken at, *x, 10, 16, 17, 22, 26, 30, 106*
processing of immigrants at, 17–18, 23–26, 28–31
restoration and reopening of, 105–106
during World War II, 82, 91
Emergency Quota Act, 84
Emergency Refugee Shelter (Fort Ontario), 91

English-only concept, 106–107
ESL (English as a Second Language), 107
ethnic communities, 72, 74–75
eugenics, 66
European migration and immigration, 7, 37–45, 52–53, 67, 69, 72
eye hooks, 26

family separations, 25, 88, 115
Feature Profile Test, 79, *79*
Filipino people, 88–89, 90
Fillmore, Millard, 50, 52
First Americans, migration of, 35–37, *36*
First Thanksgiving 1621, The (Ferris), *34*
Ford, Gerald, 101
Foreign Miners' License Act (1850), 56–57
foreign nationals, 108
442nd Regimental Combat Team, 91
Fourteenth Amendment, 62
Fox, Vicente, 109
Frank, Anne, 95, *95*
Frank, Otto, 95
French Revolution, 49

Gam Saan ("gold mountain"), 54
Georgia colony, 45
German immigrants, 50, 82–83, *83*, 95, 106
German schools, *106*
Gibbet Island, 12
gold, pull of, 54, 56–57
gold panning, 55, *56*
Governors Island, 11, 12
Greaser Law, 56
Great Depression, 85, 87
Great Hall (Ellis Island), 12
Great Hunger, 52–54
Great Hunger memorial, *52*
green card status, 108, 117
Grussman, Sinaida, 94
Gull Island, 12

Haitian refugees, 101, 103
Harlem Renaissance, 115
Harrison, Benjamin, 9, 15
Haymarket Square Riot, 66
Hessians, 48–49
Hine, Lewis, 8, 66–67, *67*
Hitler, Adolf, 66, 89
Homestead Act of 1862, 60
Honduran immigrants, 113
Hoover, Herbert, 87
Hudson, Henry, 42
Humane Borders, 112
Hungarian refugees, 100

ICE (US Immigration and Customs Enforcement), 109
Illegal Immigrant Reform and Immigrant Responsibility Act of 1996, 108, 111
Immigration Act of 1882, 65–66
Immigration Act of 1891, 12–13
Immigration Act of 1907, 72
Immigration Act of 1917, 78
Immigration Act of 1921, 84
Immigration Act of 1924, 84, 89
Immigration Act of 1990, 107–108
Immigration and Nationality Act of 1952, 96
Immigration and Nationality Act of 1965, 100–101
Immigration and Naturalization Service (INS), 88, 97
Immigration Reform and Control Act of 1986, 107
Immigration Restriction League (IRL), 67, 78
immigration stations. *See* Angel Island; Ellis Island
indentured servants, 45
intelligence tests, 66, 79
International Picnic Day, 116
internment program, Japanese, 90–91

Irish immigrants, *2*, 50, 52, 54, 61, 83
Irish Poor Law Extension Act (1847), *53*
Irish Potato Famine, 52–53

Jamestown Colony, 40, *40*, 41
Japanese immigrants, *63*, 65, 90–91
Jefferson, Thomas, 49
Jewish immigrants, 42, 44, 48, 94, 95
Johnson, Albert, 84
Johnson, Lyndon B., 100, *101*

Kennedy, John F., 100
Kindred Spirits (sculpture), 53, *53*
King George, 45
King Philip, 42
Know-Nothing party, 7, 50, 52
Knox, Howard, 66, 79
Knox Imitation Cube Test, 79
Kreyche, Mike, *112*
Ku Klux Klan, 83–84

Lady Liberty. *See* Statue of Liberty
language difficulties, 4, 20, 24, 25, 88
Lazarus, Emma, *14*
Leveroni family, *74*
LGBTQ immigrants, 78, 108
Liberty Island, 11
Lincoln, Abraham, 61
literacy tests, 69, 78
Los Samaritanos, 112
Lost Colony of Roanoke, 37, 39
Lotsky, Jacob, 30
Lyon, Matthew, 49

manifests, 3, 25, 28, *29*
Mariel boatlift, 103
Marshall, James, *54*
Massachusetts Bay Company, 42
Massasoit, *44*
Mayflower (ship), 41

Mayorkas, Alejandra N., 111
McKinley, William, 66
medical care, 18, 20–21
medical examinations, *22*, 24–28, *26*, 76
Menéndez de Avilés, Pedro, 37
mental issues, 78, 79
Metacom, 42
Mexican immigrants, 56, 65, 87, 88, 89–90, *89*, 97, 108. *See also* Bracero Program
Mexico–United States border, *104*, 111, 113, *113*, 117
Migration and Refugee Assistance Act (1962), 100
military service, 60, 82, *82*, 90, 91
minors. *See* children
Mohegan people, 12
money changers, 4
money exchange, 31, *31*, *32–33*
Moore, Annie, xi, 13, *13*, 29
mustasoles, 19

name changes, *33*
national language, lack of, 106–107
National Park Service, 53, 100
National Quarantine Act of 1893, 15–16
Native Americans, 41, 53, 57
nativism, 7, 50, 52
naturalization, 2, 49, 65
Naturalization Act of 1798, 49
Naturalization Act of 1906, 65
Navajo and Hopi Families Covid-19 Relief Fund, 53
"New Colossus, The" (Lazarus), 14
New Mexico, 56–57
New Netherland, 42, 44
New York Board of Commissioners of Emigration, 4–5, 9
New York City, 3, 5, 72
New York City Draft Riots, 61, *61*
newsies, 74, *74*

Nisei, 90–91
nurses, 18

Obama, Barack, 109, 110, 113
Oglethorpe, James Edward, 45
Olympic (ship), 69
Operation Wetback, 97
orphan trains, 72
Oyster Island, 12

Pacific Railroad Act (1862), 61–62
Page Act (1875), 62–63
Paine, Thomas, 48
Palmer Raids, 83
paper sons and daughters, 63, 76, 85
parole powers, 101
Patuxet people, 41
Penn, William, 44
Perkins, Frances, 89
Peterssen, Arne, 96–97
Pilgrims, 41–42
Plymouth Company, 40
Ponce de León, Juan, 37
potato blight, 52–53
Pozzini, Federico and Carmela (Stanga), *31*
public assistance, 65–66, 108, 117
Puck magazine, *63*
Pulaski, Casimir, *48*
pull factors, 2, 50, 54, 100
Puritans, 42
push factors, 2, 52, 113

Quakers, 44
quarantine, 5, 15
questions and questioning, 16, 28, 29–30, 76, 78
quota systems, 60, 84–85, 86, 89, 94, 96

Raleigh, Sir Walter, 37
Ramirez, Johan, 41
Reagan, Ronald, 91, 107

Red Scare, 83, 96
redemptioners, 45
Refugee Act (1980), 103
refugee camps, 91, 94–96, 103
Refugee Relief Act (1953), 96
refugees, 49, 89, 91, 94–96, 100–101, 103, 113
Registry Room (Ellis Island), 12
repatriation, 87–88
restrictionists, 69, 78, 85
Revere, Paul, 68
Riis, Jacob, 66–67
Roanoke. *See* Lost Colony of Roanoke
Roosevelt, Franklin D., 89, 90, 91
Roosevelt, Theodore, 21, 66
Russian immigrants, 69, 78, 83

Salomon, Haym, 48
Sedition Act of 1798, 49
segregation, 75, 107
77th Infantry Division, 82, *82*
Short-faced Bear and Hunters, *36*
six-second exam, 25
slavery, 40–41, 61
Smolenyak, Megan, 13
smugglers and smuggling, of immigrants, 108, 111
Society of Friends, 44
Southeast Asian refugees, 101, 103
special board of inquiry, 16
Special Immigrant Juvenile Status, 115
SS *Angelo*, *24*
St. Augustine, Florida, *37*
Statue of Liberty, 11, *15*
Statue of Liberty National Monument, 100
Statue of Liberty–Ellis Island Centennial Commission, 105–106
steamer classes, 107
steamship companies, 5, 15, 67, 69
steerage, xi, 2, 4, 24, 29
Steerage Act of 1819, 2–3, 5

steerage passengers, *3, 4, 7,* 25
Sutter, John August, 54
Sutter's Mill, *54*

Temporary Protection Status (TPS), 110–111
tenement housing, *67*
time capsules, 68
Tohono O'odham Nation, 111
Transcontinental Railroad, 61–62, 64
Treaty of Guadalupe Hidalgo (1848), 56
trough, immigration, 2
Truman, Harry, 91, 94, 95–96
Trump, Donald, 109–110, 115, 117
Tucson Samaritans, 112
Tydings-McDuffie Act (1934), 88
typhus, 5, 53

undocumented immigrants, 85, 87–89, 97, 107–110, 115, 117–118
Union Pacific Railroad, 62
US Citizenship and Immigration Services (USCIS), 108–109
US Congress, 49, 65, 78, 82, 84, 85, 107
US Constitution, 62

Vietnamese refugees, 101, 103
Virginia Company, 40
visas, 85, 89, 94, 96, 108, 109, 117

Wampanoag people, 42
War Refugee Board, 91
waves, immigration, 2
Weiss, Arnold, 78
West Indies immigrants, 115
Williams, Roger, 42
Wilson, Woodrow, 82
Windom, William, 9, 12
Women's March poster, *110*
World War I, 81–82
World War II, 90–91